WASHINGTON STATE

THE GREATEST BAND

THAT EVER WASN'T

For information about permissions to reproduce selections from this book, translation rights, or to order bulk purchases, go to www.SunyataBooks.com.

Cover photo by Danny Baird
Author photo by Tad Fettig
Book design by Bryan Tomasovich at The Publishing World

Martin, Barrett
The Greatest Band That Ever Wasn't: The Story Of The Roughest, Toughest, Most Hell-Raising Band To Ever Come Out Of The Pacific Northwest, The Screaming Trees

ISBN 978-1-0878-8153-9

1. BIOGRAPHY & AUTOBIOGRAPHY / Composers & Musicians

Printed in the U.S.A.
Distributed by Ingram

WWW.SUNYATABOOKS.COM

THE GREATEST BAND

THAT EVER WASN'T

The Story Of The Roughest, Toughest, Most Hell-Raising Band To
Ever Come Out Of The Pacific Northwest, The Screaming Trees

A COMEDY/TRAGEDY IN 3 ACTS

BARRETT MARTIN

This book is dedicated to all the great musicians with whom I have had the honor of playing music with. Most are still here, others have crossed over to the other side, but these gentlemen in particular taught me what rock & roll is all about: Mark Lanegan, Van Conner, Gary Lee Conner, Josh Homme, David Catching, Fred Drake, Jack Endino, Ben McMillan, Matt Cameron, Kim Thayil, Chris Cornell, Kurt Cobain, Krist Novoselic, Dave Grohl, Duff McKagan, Mike McCready, Stone Gossard, Jeff Ament, Eddie Vedder, Jerry Cantrell, Mike Inez, Sean Kinney, Layne Staley, and John Baker Saunders.

INTRODUCTION

Rock & roll is defiance expressed through music. And since songwriting is the main vehicle for achieving that expression, becoming a great songwriter is the ultimate practice for a rock musician. That was the primary mission of all the great bands in history, and this book is about one of those groups. Along the way, they had quite an adventure.

So many great songwriters have been forgotten to the sands of time, and it seems as if modern pop culture has wired us to forget them quickly, as the corporate media forces us to move on to the next big thing that demands our attention. You are correct if you think modern pop music is getting simpler and less original, where the songs sound more like nursery rhymes sung by a child on auto-tune, rather than the powerful, soulful compositions of decades past. Of course there are always exceptions to the trends, and many great new artists are always emerging. However, several studies have proven this downward trajectory, where modern songs use the same, tired chord progressions, with overly simplistic melodies, and a generic approach to music production that makes everything sound the same. The real problem is that mediocrity sells and it sells big, and the media corporations know this.

I think this is why musical success has been wrongly equated to financial success, rather than the artistic merit that comes from great songwriting. And since financial and artistic success are two very different things, it can also be said, and perhaps more truthfully, that the greatest artists in history are not necessarily those who accumulate wealth and fame, but those who display the highest artistic ingenuity, combined with a burning vision for something different, something much greater than themselves.

Often in these cases, if not the vast majority of the time, these artists never achieve the mainstream success of their peers, yet they blaze a trail (sometimes more akin to a scorched earth) as they display illuminated flashes of brilliance, forged in the crucible of their chosen art form. These artists create something that is lasting and far more influential than any of the flash in the pan fodder that occupies most of mainstream music. This is also why those who try mightily and fail spectacularly usually have a far more interesting story to tell than those who become wealthy by making pedestrian music and never do anything interesting or original.

This book is about a band that many people loved, who failed miserably at being a "successful rock band" in the commercial sense of the word, yet they left behind an indelible mark on American music, on their fans, and on the history of the Pacific Northwest. That band was the Screaming Trees, the greatest band that ever wasn't.

Now, the first truth of rock & roll is that it is ultimately a musical expression that pushes back against hypocritical social values, which have no real use in society except to control the minds of the youngest generation, steering them towards cultural and religious homogeneity. And since young people hate to be controlled more than just about anything, the vast majority of rock bands are started by teenagers and twenty-somethings who are rebelling against these calcified institutions. Rock music becomes their most direct countermeasure against the banality of conservative belief systems, and all the invented nonsense that goes with it. This is why the explosive music of youth can be so powerful—and also why it is sometimes feared.

This movement started in the early 1950s with the earliest of American rockers like Chuck Berry, Little Richard, Elvis Presley, and Jerry Lee Lewis, but we are now well into 70 years of rock & roll history, and much has happened in the ensuing decades, including the now legendary 1990s.

The second truth about rock music is that most rock bands have a very short shelf-life, and most never even make it out of their basements and garages to play live shows, much less tour the world. These bands exist in name only, which is why it's so perplexing that a band like the Screaming Trees, who recorded 8 studio albums during their 15 year existence and played over a thousand shows around the world, never attained the mainstream success of their peers. It is even more ironic that many thoroughly mediocre bands who arrived in the second, third, and fourth waves of the alternative music revolution would be the ones to capitalize on that originality, while those who pioneered the form often had little or nothing to show for it. Which is why the old saying still rings true:

"Do not be the first at anything—be the second."

The Screaming Trees were one of the first bands in the early alternative music scene, starting in the mid 1980s and working throughout the entirety of the 1990s. They were at the spear point of it all, while other alternative bands were still growing out their hair and trying to select which flannel shirt to match the color of their Doc Martens. Meanwhile, the Screaming Trees were blazing a musical trail that others would follow for years to come, becoming one of the most original rock bands of the last 40 years. Unfortunately, they were also one of the most self-destructive.

On any given night, the Screaming Trees could be the best live rock band in the world, and many critics have written this very thing. I can affirm that belief, having seen the Trees play long before I was even in the band, and also having seen some the best rock bands in the world. The Trees were a collection of eccentric live wires who could alternately send an audience into the stratosphere, or turn inward on itself and become as destructive as a raging bull in a china shop. This is also why it can be said that on one of those self-destructive nights, the Screaming Trees could also be one of the worst bands in the world. Consistency was not their forte, but in the realm of songwriting, the Trees had very few peers. Songwriting was their gold, it was their treasure, and what happened in between these two polarities of creation and destruction is the subject of this book.

My perspective on the Trees is unique, in that I was their longest serving drummer, joining in 1991 and staying until the band's final show in 2000. I witnessed, firsthand, the last decade of the band's 15-year existence, which was also the decade when they made their greatest albums and experienced their greatest successes.

I think I saw the band more objectively from the drum throne, because even though I became good friends with all of them, I was always a little bit on the outside looking in. This is because I didn't grow up and go to the same high school as the other Screaming Trees, in a small eastern Washington town. Instead, I grew up in another small

3

town about the same distance south as the Trees were east. We did, however, have some common perspectives, because we were all music fans in small towns where the general mentality was focused on high school football, perpetual alcoholism, and a general backwater mentality that tended to reduce the horizons of its citizens rather than expand them. That's also the very reason why musicians like the Trees find each other and form alliances to collaborate in these often dismal, rural surroundings.

You see, the Screaming Trees were ultimately a collection of misfits, albeit very smart and talented ones. Mark Lanegan was born to be one of the greatest singers of his generation; Gary Lee Conner was a naturally gifted songwriter; his brother Van Conner was a brilliant bassist with hit songwriting abilities; and I ended up being a drummer and producer who played with some of the best bands of my generation. None of this is braggadocio or exaggeration, this is just what 40 years of music history has taught us.

The counter-offensive to our individual musical abilities was our propensity for excessive drinking, various drug abuses, and serious bouts of fisticuffs with random strangers. This bizarre combination of great musicianship and songwriting skills, mixed with a pattern for addiction and self destruction is what made the Trees brilliant, yet so bedeviled in the quest for the golden ring of success. That in and of itself is not an uncommon story in rock & roll, because how many bands have told an identical tale? The difference with the Trees is that they were at the starting point of the Seattle music scene in the late 1980s, leading a charge that bands like Nirvana, Pearl Jam, Soundgarden, and Alice In Chains would later follow. All of those bands had much greater success than the Screaming Trees in the traditional sense of the word, but those bands were also some of the biggest fans of the Screaming Trees and their songs.

Our late singer and musical brother, Mark Lanegan, has already written the definitive book on the darker side of rock & roll, and none of those stories need to be retread here, nor am I interested in revisiting them. What I am interested in, however, are the more humorous and downright ridiculous situations that the band found itself in, including the qualities that made us a great band in the first place. That's where the most interesting stories are usually found—in the humor, in the levity, and in the absurdity of life on the road in a rock & roll band.

It was also brought to my attention during a conversation with one of Mark's songwriting collaborators, Duke Garwood, that I might be the longest serving musician in Mark's long and storied career. Considering that I first worked with Mark in 1991 and was working on various projects with him up until a month before his death in 2022, that becomes 30 years of an ongoing musical and literary relationship between us. Some words and stories need to be dedicated to his great talent, as well as our other departed brother, Van Conner.

Although I joined the band in 1991, five years into their run, I was already well aware of the Trees musical reputation. The original four members had come from the small eastern Washington town of Ellensburg, which was also the origin point of Stuart Anderson's Black Angus Ranch and the steakhouses that would bear his name.

I was raised in Olympia, WA, the state capitol, and like Ellensburg, it had the same economic mixture of most small towns in the Pacific Northwest: timber and agriculture, state employees, small businesses, but not much in the way of a music scene. I learned about music from inherited and purchased albums, paid for by working at a local hotel throughout high school and college. This is also why I fit right in when I joined the Trees, because we all had the same great love of music despite our humble beginnings.

After forming in 1985, the Trees had independently released their first EP, *Other Worlds* (1985), which was recorded by a local producer named Steve Fisk. They followed it up with a series of acclaimed studio albums, also produce by Fisk, that were ambitiously written, recorded, and released on two of the hippest indie labels in the world: SST Records in Long Beach, CA, and Sub Pop Records in Seattle, WA. The Trees released one album each and every year starting with the SST releases, *Clairvoyance* (1986), *Even If And Especially When* (1987), *Invisible Lantern* (1988), *Buzz Factory* (1989), their Sub Pop EP *Change Has Come* (1989), and then their first major label album, *Uncle Anesthesia* (1991).

This extraordinary outpouring of albums happened between the year I graduated from high school, 1985, and the year I had my first album out with the band Skin Yard, in 1991. In those same 7 years, the Screaming Trees had made 5 albums and two EPs, a staggering output for an indie band. They were already local legends, but the emphasis was on *local, as* the rest of the world was very slow to catch on.

Back in the 1980s, starting a band was a revolutionary idea, mostly because the average person would never consider dropping out of mainstream society to take such a radically different path. Normal people graduated from high school, went to college, and landed regular jobs. People who started a band, on the other hand, were completely strange and way off the traditional career map. Yet being in a band was alluring and even exotic in a certain kind of way. It was like being a pirate in a society that scorned the pirate, but secretly wanted to be him at the same time.

Nowadays, everyone and their parents are in a band, and we even have summer camps and schools of rock that teach kids how to be rock musicians. I'm fine with that actually—music should never be exclusionary or elitist, and I've always believed that everyone should play a musical instrument just for the joy of it. But back in the 1980s, starting a band and doing everything on our own, with nothing but old records to guide our way—that was a very different approach to life. It was a real commitment, and that's how we invented an alternative way of making music.

Our starting point was Seattle in the late 1980s, and back then Seattle was a working class city with a cross section of the same economic demographics as our small towns, just on a larger scale. Yet there was something magical happening in the Seattle underground, including a bohemian approach to art, film, and music that just kept growing, like the psychedelic mushrooms that sprout in abundance every autumn across the Pacific Northwest.

Young people started moving to Seattle by the van load, and every club in the city was pumping out new music every night of the week. The Internet wouldn't exist for another decade, and Facebook invites wouldn't come for another 20 years, so everything back then was word of mouth, which is a kind of wildfire in its own way. It only cost about $2.00 to see a show, so the social life of a young Seattleite was largely determined by the bands whose shows they attended, and the audience those bands attracted. That's where we met our friends, our girlfriends, and our future band mates.

It was exciting to be young, to be in the middle of such massive creativity, especially as a musician. I moved to Seattle for the first time in the summer of 1986, and then permanently in the fall of 1987, maintaining a residence there until about 2018.

Between 1987 and 1991, I played in two Seattle rock bands while supporting myself as a carpenter for a small Seattle home construction company. I also did a short stint working in the Sub Pop Records mail room, although at Sub Pop, I was only paid with vinyl.

My first band was a punk group called Thin Men, and we essentially modeled ourselves after The Clash, in the sense that we had punk clothes, short hair, and even shorter songs. They were good, original songs though, and that helped us build a small but loyal following. We played from Bellingham in the north, to Portland, OR in the south, and we recorded one cassette-only album titled, *A Round Hear* (1988).

Thin Men actually opened for the Screaming Trees in 1988, at the same college I had attended in Bellingham when I was a music student at Western Washington University. The Trees had only been a band for a couple of years at that point, but I was awestruck by their explosive live show. I remember talking to guitarist Gary Lee Conner after the show, and asking him about their experience being on SST Records, which had released albums from many of my favorite bands. We all knew something revolutionary was happening in our part of the country, and the Trees were at the forefront of it all.

The second band I joined was a much more successful group than the first, and they had been around for about the same amount of time as the Screaming Trees. They were called Skin Yard, and they had been founded by guitarist-producer, Jack Endino, who is fondly referred to as the Godfather of Grunge, because of his production work on early recordings from bands like Soundgarden, Mudhoney, Nirvana, and the Screaming Trees. Jack had also recorded my drum tracks during a Thin Men recording session that I had convinced him to produce in 1989, and a few days later he called to ask me to play drums on his solo album. This eventually led to me joining Skin Yard the following year in 1990, and that changed my life forever.

Skin Yard had already recorded three albums and toured across North America before I ever joined the band, and during my tenure as their drummer, we made two more albums. Those albums made the band experience its highest watermark with the albums, *1000 Smiling Knuckles* (1991), which peaked at #2 on the college radio chart, and *Inside The Eye,* which was released posthumously in 1993. We also did a series of tours across North America and Europe, in between which I continued to work as a house-building carpenter. Thus, my days as a carpenter, and my nights as a rock drummer were completely full, while I lived the life I had always wanted to live—as a recording, touring musician. Music didn't pay my bills yet, and I hardly had time to sleep, but I was incredibly happy for the first time in my young life. And even though I was only in Skin Yard for about two years, it was the greatest two years of my life up to that point.

Upon Skin Yard's return from our one and only European tour in the fall of 1991, I got a call from my friend, Kim White, who at the time was vice president of marketing and alternative promotion at Geffen Records, where Nirvana had just released their groundbreaking album, *Nevermind (1991)*. Kim told me that the Screaming Trees needed to find a permanent replacement for original drummer Mark Pickerel, who had finally left the band. The Trees had had a series of substitute drummers over the years, the most recent being Dan Peters, the drummer for Mudhoney. Dan was about to return to Mudhoney to record their next album, so the Trees needed to find a permanent drummer, to record and tour over the long haul, and that's when I was asked to audition.

This is how my tenure in the Trees began, and this is also where the 33 short stories in this book begin to tell the tale of our Odyssean adventure. Because that is exactly what it felt like to be a Screaming Tree— it was like a Greek myth, complete with unbelievable circumstances, cyclopean nemeses, captivating sirens, and like Odysseus himself, the journey lasted almost exactly 10 years. I think you'll find that within these firsthand stories and historical reflections, a more objective and personal understanding of our band.

As I said at the beginning of this introduction, the Trees were really a group of brilliant misfits who often made mistakes, both individually and collectively. But we also wrote several albums of great songs that inspired many other bands. Ultimately when it was finally over, we came to love each other as brothers who had been bonded in the crucible of extreme experience, which is what every great band goes through at some point in their career. This book is about those extreme experiences, the laughter that wouldn't stop, and some of the more outright dangerous situations we found ourselves in.

I started writing these stories back in 2015, at the same time that I was writing my first book, *The Singing Earth (2017)*. I had written several stories about the Screaming Trees, which I intended to include in that book, but because I had to limit the number of stories, most of the best ones remained unpublished. Then Mark Lanegan called to ask me about my own memories of the Trees when he was writing his memoir. We both laughed hysterically at what we could remember, and not remember, and Mark encouraged me to tell my side of the saga with an emphasis on humor. We all knew that comedy is the best platform for these kinds of stories, because comedy is really just tragedy—plus time.

Sadly, with the passing of Mark in 2022, and then the passing of Van in 2023, I decided that these stories needed to be finished and shared with our fans and the greater public. I want people to remember the Trees as the star-crossed brothers that we were, who saw an opportunity to escape a dull life in our respective small towns, to make music, and to see the greater world.

So with that being said, I want to emphasize that this book is a tribute to all my musical brothers, from all the bands I have been in over the years, especially for those who left us early. The music we made together still remains as a corpus of the best singers and songwriters of our generation.

All of these stories are true and written as accurately as I possibly could, and they have been read and corroborated by other people who were present and witness to these events. I have written them just as I personally experienced them, with as much historical accuracy as could be found. The people who read various drafts of this book are people who either worked with the Trees or played music with us, and they have given me their comments and opinions, which I have included in the final text. I want to thank those people directly and offer my deepest gratitude for their comments and contributions. They are: Gary Lee Conner, Kim White, Lisette Garcia, Peter Buck, Duff McKagan, Mike McCready, Duke Garwood, Jason Everman, and Bryan Tomasovich, who also did the layout and design of this book.

My sincerest hope is that these stories will remind people why rock & roll is such an important part of American musical history, and why great songwriting is still one of the highest forms of artistic expression ever invented by human beings.

All of this is really just a dream, a kind of invented reality that we're all creating together, and none of it lasts very long.

Because in order to tell a great story, you have to live it, first.

ACT I

ASCENSION

THE AUDITION

By the time I officially auditioned for the Screaming Trees, I had earned my stripes in the early Seattle music scene with Thin Men and Skin Yard. Thin Men was a more punk-oriented group, and as a result, we didn't quite fit in against the backdrop of the grunge movement that was taking over Seattle at the time. However, we had very good songs and we gigged around Washington State for a couple years, so I got my first taste of what it was like to write and record original songs, play them live, and see the audiences react to our songs. In many ways, playing with Thin Men was a great way for me to learn those basic skills.

Right before I departed that band, I had the idea to gain us some "grunge traction" by recording a single with Sub Pop producer, Jack Endino. Jack was recording every single band on Sub Pop and he had just recorded Nirvana's debut album, *Bleach*, which he sent to Sub Pop with the instructions to, "Sign this band immediately!"

Unfortunately, Thin Men's attempted two-song single was never released, largely because of the band's inability to raise enough money to press a vinyl single out of the excellent mixes that Jack had made for us. Fortunately for me, Jack really liked my drumming style, to the degree that he invited me to join his new solo project, Earthworm. That initial recording session on Jack's solo album led to me joining his regular band, Skin Yard, and this became my second Seattle band, one that was definitely *grunge*.

It was now 1990, and I had been living in Seattle since 1987—three years into my fledgling music career. For the next two years, 1990-91, I recorded and toured a great deal with Skin Yard, playing on their two best-selling albums, we did several tours around North America and one extensive tour of Europe, where we played to much larger audiences than we ever did in the United States. We even had major label interest near the end of the band, which was becoming ubiquitous for any band that was from Seattle at the time. Fortunately, we declined the various offers that came in, because Skin Yard was an indie band to its core, and all bands must eventually come to an end. Jack wanted to return to production work full time, and the rest of us knew that the band's time was up. We amicably broke up on the flight home from London on that first and only European tour in October and November of 1991.

It was now around Thanksgiving in 1991 and I was officially bandless again. I called my old foreman at the house building company and was back at work almost immediately, doing concrete foundations and carpentry, as I always did between the tours I had done up to that point. It was good, rewarding work that taught me a lot about work ethics and how to build things properly, which had countless metaphors when it came time to build bands and albums of music in the future. But I didn't want to be a carpenter forever, at least not for a paycheck, and I knew that I was destined to be a working musician. I was just thinking about who and where my next band would materialize, post Skin Yard.

Unexpectedly, the call to audition for the Screaming Trees came not more than a couple weeks after that final Skin Yard tour. I had just gotten home from a day of pouring concrete for a house foundation, my arms still splattered with mud and flecks of concrete. The initial call came from my friend Kim White at Geffen Records, who had become a good friend of both Skin Yard and the Screaming Trees. It was Kim who had introduced me to the Trees bassist, Van Conner, about a year earlier, when he had come to see Skin Yard at a club called *Bogart's* in Long Beach, California.

Bogart's was kind of a local club for the label, SST Records, which had signed Skin Yard and was also based in Long Beach. Van Conner was on tour playing bass for Dinosaur Jr., which was also on SST Records, and from our initial conversation at the club, Van was seriously considering leaving the Trees to permanently join Dinosaur Jr.

At that first meeting, Van was kind of giggling and he acted a bit goofy, which surprised me considering his giant physical stature. However we immediately connected at the soul level when he informed me that he was on psychedelic mushrooms, and he was peaking when Skin Yard played our set. If you knew Van the way I came to know this gentle giant, it made perfect sense, and I think in that moment we knew we were going to be friends, long before the audition for the Screaming Trees ever came up in his phone call.

Weirdly, the day after Van called me to audition for the Trees, I got another call from Kurt Danielson, bassist for the heaviest band in Seattle, TAD. They were also auditioning drummers. In truth, I loved both band's music because TAD appealed to my love of heavy, metal-ish rock, and the Trees appealed to my love of great songwriting. Thus, I agreed to do both auditions, which happened to be in the same building—a steel foundry in the southern, industrial part of Seattle that also happened to have rehearsal spaces. This was because the foundry's owner loved rock & roll, so he transformed an empty building at the foundry into several rehearsal studios. It was a brilliant business model because steel making and rock & roll are two of the greatest forms of American industry.

My first audition that week was with TAD, and if you know their music at all, you know that it is exceedingly loud and heavy. I liked the way their music made me feel, because it hit me hard in the chest, yet it also had a vibrant musicality that I didn't expect. My style of drumming worked very well with them and they offered me the job the same night. But I told them I needed to think about it, without telling them that I still had an audition with the Trees.

A couple days later I auditioned for the Trees, with Van on bass and his brother Gary Lee on guitar. Mark Lanegan was not present yet. We mostly played their newest songs, which they were working on for their next album. I remember playing an early version of, "Shadow Of The Season," which is one of the heaviest songs the Trees ever wrote. I had brought a gigantic Chinese crash cymbal to the audition that was about 27" inches in diameter. I had been using it in Skin Yard and it was visually huge and extremely loud, and I started hitting it on the accents in the intro part of, "Shadow Of The Season." This totally frightened Van and made him exclaim, "Jesus Christ, that thing is fucking loud!" I realized that maybe I needed to tone it down a bit and not blow my audition with one particular cymbal, but I guess the giant cymbal worked because those "frightening accents" became a pivotal part of the song when we eventually recorded it a few months later.

I was offered the drum spot in the Trees the same night, just as I had been with TAD. And I say this because in the ensuing decades, I auditioned for several other bands that were also looking for drummers, bands like R.E.M., Soundgarden, and The Black Crowes, but I was never chosen for those bands. To this day, it was only the Screaming Trees and TAD that offered me a drumming job, so in that way, fate intervened on my behalf.

I absolutely loved the Trees music, it was both heavy and beautiful, in the same way that bands like Black Sabbath and Led Zeppelin had a kind of dark beauty in their music. And with me on drums and Van on bass, the Trees developed a deep swing in our music that was similar to the way Sabbath and Zeppelin had their swing.

After I accepted the Trees offer, I had to phone Kurt Danielson of TAD and tell him that I had chosen the Trees. In my mind, I knew that the Trees were the best songwriters, in fact, that's what they were known for—they were becoming known as the best songwriters in Seattle. At the same time, a majority of Seattle bands were subscribing to the belief that heavy, plus loud, equals good music. However, those bands never learned a principle lesson, which is that heavy music has little to do with volume. Heavy music is built around chord structure, lyrics, and rhythmic delivery, so a great, heavy song can often be played with acoustic instruments, as the band Alice In Chains did so expertly.

I knew within 15 minutes of playing with the Trees that they had all of the qualities of the best rock bands in history—they were songwriting bad asses with an emphasis on a powerful, heavy delivery, and now with a deep swing in the rhythm section to back it up. Of course, the Trees could be as loud as they wanted to be, but it was always about the songs, first and foremost.

Van, Lee, and I immediately launched into our first few weeks of rehearsals, and they soon changed locations when they saw my warehouse loft on Jackson Street, in Seattle's International district. My loft was much nicer than the rehearsal space at the steel foundry. I had a thousand square feet of bright, sunlit space with a refrigerator, a coffee maker, a large couch, and a bathroom. I lived there too, and even though I didn't have any money, I made my loft into a really cool space for musicians to hang out and play music. It was luxurious accommodations for any rock band, and the Trees became the third band to rehearse and write songs there after the Thin Men and Skin Yard.

Things were improving in my musical life and I was back in a band, once again.

A LUSTY LADY

As the Trees continued to rehearse as a trio, I had sort of assumed that Mark Lanegan had done his due diligence on my musical background, perhaps asking Jack Endino about my qualities as a drummer and potential band mate. Apparently he had not, because one day Mark randomly showed up at my loft for Trees rehearsal. I was suddenly very nervous, even though I had been playing the new songs for about two or three weeks at that point, so I had a fairly firm grasp on the Trees style. Mark didn't sing as we rehearsed that day, however he did sit on the couch and sip a couple beers, listening attentively to what we were creating. He would occasionally nod his head in silent approval, sometimes correcting what Lee or Van might be playing on a given song. But it became clear that Mark was really listening to the songs, and I could tell from his face that he very much liked what we were creating.

Mark offered musical advice as the evolution of the songs took place in real time, and he had a rare ability to recognize a great idea at its inception point, which could then be shaped into something original and powerful. He also recognized and ardently avoided the minefield of old, bloated cliches that every rock band must vigilantly watch out for. "That sounds steakhouse!" Mark would occasionally exclaim, perhaps a reference to those Black Angus restaurants that had come from his hometown. We stayed as far away as we could from anything that sounded remotely steakhouse, and I'm sure you can guess what that might be.

I imagined that Mark was working out lyrics and melodies as we played the songs, and Lee would occasionally sing a scratch vocal part that he had written for the demo because up to this point, Lee had been the main songwriter for the Trees. As I came to learn about the band's creative process over the years, Mark was often working on his lyrical and melodic ideas, long before he would attempt to step up to the microphone and sing them with the band. He was working it out in his head, while we physically worked it out with our instruments.

During that first rehearsal with Mark, he seemed very happy with the progress we had made on the approximately 15 songs that we were developing for the next album. This was also the beginning of a time when Mark had started drinking alcohol again after many years of sobriety. In fact, my knowledge of Mark prior to this was that he was a sober guy, as I also was at the time. Mark told me later that he had started drinking again after an incident on a previous tour, when the Trees rolled their van on the freeway with Mark inside the van. It had happened on their North American tour when Dan Peters of Mudhoney was sitting in as their temporary drummer, about a year before I joined the band. After that experience of near death, Mark decided to go back to drinking. I kept it to myself, but I thought it was an odd decision to start drinking again, since near death experiences usually make people go in the opposite direction, towards sobriety. Maybe his rational was that if you're already sober when death comes near, then drinking is somewhat of a pressure valve. Regardless of the rational, I think the van rolling incident was the beginning of Mark's infamously dark adventure, one that I occasionally joined in from time to time.

At this time, however, I wasn't drinking yet because I was always careful not to even drink a single beer if I was working on music, playing a show, and definitely not if I had to drive after the show. My philosophy was largely formed from my previous years playing with Thin Men and Skin Yard, where various band members often played drunk or stoned, and the musical magic never ignited. And not to sound overly cautious, but I cared about how I played as a drummer and the way it affected people, and playing sober was always the best model for me. I still hadn't made a name for myself, and I wasn't going to let drinking interfere with that process. Unfortunately, as my life in the Trees rolled forward, my own drinking problem would emerge, and it was much to my own detriment.

At the end of that first Trees rehearsal with Mark, we began wrapping up for the night, and Van and Lee began to pack up their guitars. That's when Mark announced to me (or rather demanded) that I accompany him to *The Lusty Lady*, a kind of kitschy, strip tease theater modeled after the old time peep shows of the early 20th century. *The Lusty Lady* was actually owned and operated by an all-women business group, and they prided themselves on the fact that no men owned or operated their establishment. They were happy to take your money though, as long as everyone behaved.

Looking back on it, it seems like a fairly innocent thing, but to be honest, I think I had only been in a strip club twice in my life—once for a friend's bachelor party, which was so cliché it was stupid, and once at a strip club/restaurant in Manitoba, Canada, where Skin Yard had mistakenly stopped for dinner. We were about to eat our hamburgers and fries when a completely naked dancer came dancing across the top of bar. That was our experience in rural Canada.

Although I had walked past it a hundred times going to clubs in downtown Seattle, I had never even been inside *The Lusty Lady*. I figured if I was going to go, it might as well be with Mark Lanegan as my personal escort. I was not a naïve person by any stretch, and I'd already traveled or toured across three continents, including North America, Europe, and Australia. But I wasn't experienced in very many things other than building houses, playing music, and touring in a van with a bunch of dudes. I had two years of college and 4 years playing in rock bands under my belt, but strip clubs weren't a big thing on my radar.

The main reason why Mark wanted to go to *The Lusty Lady* in the first place was because he wanted to see a visiting porn star, who he had discovered during his many years working at the Conner brothers family video store in Ellensburg. This particular starlet, whose name I will not mention, was doing a live, in-person performance. So off we went, Mark driving the two of us in his beige 1962 Plymouth Valiant, which had been given to him by Kurt Cobain of the now globally famous, Nirvana.

We looked for a parking spot on 1st Avenue in downtown Seattle, and this was back when Seattle actually had ample street parking, and nobody really went downtown except to see a show. Back then, downtown Seattle was relatively dead, and you could drive from one end of the city to the other, in any direction, in the span of about 15 minutes.

This was a time when people were actually leaving Seattle to move to San Francisco and Los Angeles, not the other way around. Now it takes at least an hour to drive across the city in its infamously gridlocked traffic, and newer Seattleites probably wouldn't believe that this era of easy driving and parking ever existed. Indeed it did, and that's part of the reason why a gigantic music scene got going here in the first place.

By the time we arrived at *The Lusty Lady,* Mark was fairly tipsy from the beer drinking at rehearsal, but he was still in a convivial mood, laughing and displaying the affable personality that those of us who knew him would occasionally see. I liked Mark immediately, he seemed like a fun person to hang out with, so into the theatre we went, paying the small entrance fee to watch the striptease of the aforementioned starlet. I was unimpressed, but then again, what did I expect?

After the striptease, I felt like it was time to leave, because even though *The Lusty Lady* was owned and operated by women, hanging around for too long starts to feel a bit like hanging around in the kitchen of a greasy diner after Friday dinner rush, another job I previously worked, which is why I took up carpentry instead. I had to get out of there.

Mark wanted to stay however, he had other business to attend to, so I started walking back to Jackson Street, to the relative sanctity of my loft. It was a good first day with Mark, which included playing new songs, having some laughs, and then a rather laddish time at the local strip club. You might think this is a politically incorrect thing for the judgmental times in which we now live, but I think we can all agree that there are much worse things happening than musicians going to a strip club. My trip to *The Lusty Lady* seems quite innocent by comparison.

And that was my first date with Mark Lanegan. It was literally sex, drugs, and rock & roll—in reverse order.

SWEET OBLIVION

It was now January of 1992, and the Trees were getting ready to record their sixth studio album, which was also their second album for their major label, Epic Records. For me, it was only the 4th album I had ever played on up to that point in my life. None of us knew what kind of album we were going to make, but we knew we had some truly great songs to start with.

The rehearsals we had done in my Jackson Street loft over the previous two months had a fierce, energetic quality to them. I think this was partly due to my drumming style, and also my influence as a new member of the band. Guitarist Gary Lee compared my drumming style with the Trees original drummer, Mark Pickerel, when he said, "Pickerel plays bombastically, kind of like Keith Moon of The Who, whereas you play much groovier, like John Bonham of Led Zeppelin." Both of those legendary drummers are exceptional in their style and influence, and I suppose Gary Lee's comparisons can be taken as compliments to both Mark Pickerel and myself.

I had been developing my style for years by then, which started with my training as a jazz drummer in high school and college, and then a much heavier approach when I started playing rock & roll with Jack Endino and Skin Yard. I found that I loved all forms of music that had a groove in them, and the best of those songs also had swing, so I made that my dual focus—our songs must have groove and swing. And if I really boil it down to the essential qualities in my drumming, I'd say that those two things are my best strengths.

We had rehearsed diligently during those two months in the fall and early winter of 1991-92, with Mark finally starting to sing his evolving lyrics as the songs progressed. Our approach was to go through each song methodically, checking the arrangements and perfecting all the little twists and turns that make a song unique—a drop out in the drums here, a guitar riff that answers a vocal melody there, an introduction that sets up the entire mood of the song, or an outro that concluded it, these were the small but hugely important things that we examined with scientist-like meticulism. In the down time when we were just hanging out or taking a break to drink coffee or smoke a cigarette, we would talk about our individual music influences and the production ideas we wanted to try out when it finally came time to record the album. We were thinking way forward.

Sometime in late January of 1992, we had a meeting with Bob Pfeifer, our A&R rep from Epic Records. Bob flew out to Seattle to observe us as we recorded demos for all the new songs during a whirlwind, one-day session at Seattle's Avast Studios. The session was produced by Jack Endino, who became a lifelong friend and my first musical mentor. Jack had also produced a previous Trees album, *Buzz Factory* (1989), which was one of my favorite Trees albums. Under Jack's quick yet careful production skills, we knocked out the vast majority of the songs in one day, doing live, single takes, the result of our months of rehearsing. Suddenly our songs, which had working titles that were absurdly ridiculous and even offensive, came together as presentable songs.

For example, the triumphant chorus for the song, "Troubled Times," was no longer sung as, "Shit my pants on Monday, now I got to hurry," and was now elegantly re-phrased to be, "Booked and I got to hurry, troubled times and worry."

Another song, "Dollar Bill," had the tag line originally sung as "Queer as a three dollar bill" but was corrected to, "Torn like an old dollar bill."

It's important for me to emphasize that the Trees were actually very well-read, literate guys, and we were not bigots or homophobes. But sometimes a certain lyric would emerged in the writing of a song, and we would laugh so damn hard every time that irreverent chorus went by, that it was hard to change the words to be acceptable, proper lyrics. I'm sure many hit songwriters have stumbled upon this same realization, where the most absurd and offensive lyric becomes the biggest hook in the song. It's hard to change it.

You see, this was the linguistical humor of the Screaming Trees, we made up ridiculous lyrics until we had the real ones, and this became the bands inside humor, as future stories will reveal. We also had to submit legitimate, acceptable demos to our record label if we were going to get our next album advance.

The day after that fast and furious recording session, Bob took us out to dinner and told us what was happening at Epic. He thought our new songs sounded great, but there was a small hiccup, largely due to the fact that the Trees' previous album, *Uncle Anesthesia* (1991) hadn't sold very well. Even though it was a great album, it had only sold about 50,000 copies, which was puny by major label standards. Still, that was twice as much as any of the previous albums the Trees had sold on SST Records. By indie standards, 50,000 units sold is a massive number, but the album had been co-produced by Chris Cornell, the singer of Soundgarden, who was also a fan of the Trees, so Epic expected much bigger sales figures. They considered *Uncle Anesthesia* to be a commercial failure.

Chris Cornell was on his way to becoming a huge rock star, and he was an early believer in the Trees songwriting skills, which is why he wanted to co-produce their major label debut. Another issue was that other Seattle bands like Nirvana and Pearl Jam had eclipsed the Trees early success, and were now selling albums by the millions. The Trees, for their part, had signed their major label deal before any of those other bands even had an offer, and they had opened up a lot of new musical ground for these other bands. But the Trees were selling albums by the tens of thousands, whereas everyone else was selling hundreds of thousands and even millions of albums. The Trees were doing great by the indie standards we had all come up with, but they were commercially terrible under the major label standards we now had to meet. The Trees had yet to deliver a truly successful album, so we really were in a make-or-break situation. Bob Pfeifer told us this in no uncertain terms, and if we didn't make one hell of a great album, with hit songs that sold a lot records, we would likely be dropped from the label and that would almost certainly be the end of the Screaming Trees.

Thus, my first album with the Trees was also the first major label album I had ever played on, and it was also looking like it could be my last. I had joined the Trees with the odds of an underdog, a metaphor that I have always kept close to my heart, and which very aptly applied to our band. That's because when the underdog has the odds stacked against him, he has to work twice as hard to overcome them. Everyone is betting against him, yet some part of them is secretly hoping the underdog will triumph in the end. That's the power of the underdog—the power that comes from within, to overcome the odds.

A couple weeks after submitting our one-day demo session to Epic, we got the official green light—they loved the songs and our recording budget had been approved, which if I remember correctly was about $150,000. That seems like a huge amount of money now, compared to the extremely low budgets of the average 21st century recording contract, but in 1992, that was a relatively small budget to make an album for a major label—but we were damn happy to get it.

We began packing up our gear to have everything shipped to New York, and since we didn't own any professional road cases yet, everything we had was packed inside giant wooden crates. These crates looked like something you might see on an 19th century steamship, with black stenciled words on the side that said "Screaming Trees/Baby Monsters Studio, New York, NY." I put my personal belongings in a small storage unit, and I officially gave notice that I would be vacating my Jackson Street loft where so many great songs had been written. It was now February of 1992, it was the end of the early grunge era, which had lasted from1987 to 1992. However it was also the beginning of an entirely new era in Seattle rock history—the globalized, commercial success of grunge.

The Trees flew to New York City on a direct flight from SeaTac to JFK, and the following day we met up with a producer that Kim White had scouted to help us make the record. His name was Don Fleming, and he was part of the Sonic Youth team based in New York. Don also had an engineer that he liked to work with named John Agnello, so the package was complete. We all converged at the studio Don had picked out for us called *Baby Monsters*, which was located on 14th street in the Chelsea district of lower west Manhattan. The studio was rustic, as warehouse studios tend to be, and I was initially surprised at how small it appeared. But the studio had many vintage guitars and amps, and there was enough space in the tracking room to get a good, cracking drum sound, so I knew we'd be OK.

We started setting up our gear on the very first day, unpacking the giant wooden crates that were so beat up, they looked like they had gone around Cape Horn on a clipper ship to get here. By the second day, we were recording the first basic tracks. The sessions flowed naturally and they were hot, being very tight and focused, like the intense New York energy that surrounded us. We would record for several hours at a time, rehearsing a song to get it exactly right, and then we would record it immediately thereafter, while it was still fresh in our minds. Around midnight we'd wrap up for the night, breaking off into groups of two or three at a time to grab a taxi back to our hotel, the legendary Gramercy Park Hotel.

Back in 1992, the Gramercy Park Hotel was not the super expensive, uber luxurious hotel that it is today. It had once been a glamorous hotel in the 1920s and that was its heyday, but by the 1990s, it was a rather dingy and rundown affair, which was all that the Trees could afford. Van and I roomed together because we got along very well from the start—we were the rhythm section after all. We often joked that we might catch Legionnaires disease as we languished in our dank room, which veered from being shivering cold, to scorching hot when the steam radiator randomly screamed and hissed itself to life. Thus, we rarely spent much time in our room except to sleep and take a shower, choosing instead to roam the streets of Manhattan whenever we weren't in the studio.

Conveniently, the Gramercy's best feature was its downstairs bar, which was a watering hole for every rock band that happened to be passing through New York. Everyone made a stop at the Gramercy Hotel Bar, it was a required destination point, and every night after the Trees returned from a session at *Baby Monsters*, we'd have a nightcap (or several) before retiring to our rooms of gloom. Almost every single night we'd run into someone from another band we had known from our previous years on the road—Mudhoney, Sonic Youth, Nick Cave, The Fluid, and countless other musicians made a stop there. These gatherings would lead to long nights of highly animated and exaggerated storytelling, and certainly some outright lying. Such was the bravado of the young, Generation X musicians—the alternative generation.

I remember a lot of laughing in that bar, the clinking of glasses, and a room so thick with cigarette smoke that it seemed more like a cowboy saloon from the Wild West than a hipster bar in 1990s Manhattan. And when I look back at the four weeks we spent recording our album, what I remember most is the tracking room at *Baby Monsters*, the Gramercy Hotel Bar, and the pizza joint across the street, whose $1.00 slices kept us alive.

Perhaps the single most important tool we used in the making of our album, was the philosophy that we applied to each of our songs as we recorded them. We always believed that the most important thing was to serve the spirit of the song, whatever that meant, and whatever that required. Usually this spirit meant simplifying your parts and playing with more feel, rather than a technically perfect, overly-complicated part. I remember that Don Fleming didn't let me use a click track for any of the songs, because he thought it might be too mechanical for a band like the Trees. Instead, the band would follow my natural tempos as they ebbed and flowed, and this made the music come alive. You can hear that feeling in the songs, the breathing, the waiting, and then the acceleration of the band's explosive power, like a sprinter taking off at the starting line.

We always recorded the rhythm tracks live as a band, with Mark singing a scratch vocal as he sang along, which he would later re-sing after we had built up the tracks. We usually got the basic track within the first three or four takes because we were so well rehearsed from those months in my Seattle loft. Sometimes it was even the first or second take that had the magic we wanted, and we'd often keep it, even if there was a slight mistake. That's because we were recording with 24 tracks on 2" magnetic tape, and with tape, you have to make a decision after each performance if that was "the take" or not. If you decided to try again, you lost that take when you recorded over it during the next attempt. That's the magic and the gamble of magnetic tape recording— do you have the ears and the intuition to pick the best take right after you recorded it? That's a lost art form in the age of computer-generated perfection—knowing a great performance when you hear it for the first time.

A great basic track, even with a slight mistake or flaw, always has more life and character than a technically perfect performance that lacks soul. And that's because a great song should represent life itself, full of mistakes, flaws, and the imperfect souls we all carry. As every Screaming Trees fan knows, the Trees were all about the soul of a song, and that became our benchmark—does the song have soul or not?

A lot of music I hear nowadays seems to have forgotten this most important principle, soul, which is why I am emphasizing it again now. Soul is the only thing that really matters in a great song, no matter what the musical genre is.

After our basic tracks were picked, which was usually based on my drum performances and was always a continuous take, we'd fix any of the mistakes in Van's bass lines and Lee's rhythm guitar tracks. Lee would then do a couple guitar overdubs, but not much more than that. Usually he'd only play a second guitar part with a melodic lead or a solo, then I would record some simple hand percussion, like a tambourine or a shaker. After all that, Mark would sing his final vocal performance, which was meticulously edited together by our engineer, John Agnello. Then it was time to do backing vocals, the final step in the recording process.

Our producer, Don, had a theory that a small amount of whiskey helped to warm up the vocal chords and put a little growl in the vocals. Anytime Mark had to do lead vocals, or when the rest of us had to do backing vocals, Don would give us a small amount of whiskey, about half of a shot glass. Don's preferred brand was *Dimple Pinch*, but the funny thing was that Mark didn't even like whiskey. He almost exclusively drank gin and tonics, so drinking the *Dimple Pinch* was kind of an ordeal for Mark—but he drank it, and indeed, it made his vocals sound incredible.

Credit must be given to Don and his whiskey theory, because Mark's vocal performances are arguably some of the best in his long and varied career. That ancient voice, combined with the band's bullwhip-tight musical delivery, is what gives that album its classic, timeless quality.

As we were finishing the final overdubs on the last few songs, the mixes started coming back from Andy Wallace's studio across town. Andy had mixed in the previous year, Nirvana's *Nevermind (1991)*, Jeff Buckley's *Grace (1991)*, and a slew of other brilliant albums that had been hugely influential in the exploding genre of alternative music. Andy definitely had the golden ear, and when we heard his first mix for the song, "No One Knows," we knew right away that we had a very special album on our hands.

Andy mixed about two songs a day over the ensuing week, including all of the extra songs that didn't make the album, the B-Sides. When he finished, the mixes were sent over to Epic inside the Sony Blackrock building to get the final approval. Word came back that the label was extremely excited about the songs, all of the mixes were approved, and the band felt a huge sense of relief. It appeared that the hangman of dropped major label bands would not be getting his silver coin after all.

A few weeks later, we returned to New York to master the album with Howie Weinberg, a well-known mastering engineer who liked to master his albums at full volume. Needless to say, Howie's methodology suited our music extremely well, and the 11 songs that we picked for the album were sequenced and prepared for CD and LP manufacturing. I'll never forget how good the album sounded in Howie's mastering suite, it was just.....massive.

On our flight back to Seattle, the label sent a stretch limo to pick up the band and drive us from our hotel in Manhattan to the JFK airport, and Mark insisted that we play (extremely loudly) a cassette of the mastered album on the limo's stereo. We bobbed our heads as the music blared, shouting above the roar at how great it sounded. We were stoked, all of us, together in a union that only a real band can understand.

We gave our album the title of *Sweet Oblivion*, taken from a lyric in the opening song, "Shadow Of The Season," in which Mark sings, "Ahhh sweet oblivion feels alright!" It was a perfectly appropriate title because we had been living the oblivion lifestyle for the last few months, as we jetted back and forth between Seattle and New York, playing the occasional show or mini tour, recording late into the night, and then drinking until the sun rose. That feeling of fearless abandon is deeply embedded in the soul of that album, as well as the spirit of New York City.

It was now the spring of 1992, and Epic had decided on a September release date for the album, about six months later. This gave us time to start making videos for the various singles, of which we ultimately made four videos. This in turn gave Epic more tools to promote the album, but the problem with expensive videos is that the Trees had to pay back 50% of the production costs. Back then, the average music video cost about $100,000 to make, which was almost as much as making an album.

At one point, some crackpot video director, who had been hired to make a video for us, had rented a helicopter to film multiple shots that never even made it into the video—but it blew all of our gear over. This was the kind of financial waste and recklessness that these so-called directors took advantage of during the 1990s heyday of video making. This whole financial scheme was like working for the company store, where the more videos we made for the label, the more we were becoming indebted to them. By the time the album was finished and the four videos were made, we were in debt to Epic Records and their parent company, Sony Music, to the tune of half a million dollars. This was a pattern that became more and more ingrained in the Trees financial decisions, and this is also why the vast majority of major label bands never make it—because the major label business model is designed to keep you in debt.

Epic decided to release our first single, "Nearly Lost You," as part of the *Singles* movie soundtrack, which they were also releasing. The soundtrack had already been mastered and set for release by the time Kim White heard about it, but she somehow managed to get "Nearly Lost You" added to the soundtrack at the very last minute, which required that the label change the sequence and re-master the album. It was a wise decision on their part because the album turned out to be much bigger than the movie, largely because of the exploding fame of all the Seattle bands on the soundtrack, all of which made "Nearly Lost You" one of the hit songs on the soundtrack, reaching #12 on the mainstream rock chart. Even then-president, Bill Clinton, used the bridge section of "Nearly Lost You," which is a tribalistic drumbeat I created, as the background music for his inauguration on the presidential stage.

It was a surreal time to say the least, and the Trees subsequently hit the road for two straight years of touring, across three continents and countless American, European, and Australian shows.

When I listen to *Sweet Oblivion* today, the first thing I hear is the power of the performances, the shifting, breathing of the tempos, the ferociousness of the musical delivery, and the emotional tension and release of the songs. Mark's vocals roar and howl with the soul of a man much older than the 27 years he was at the time. He sang stories that were both majestic and spiritual, and haunting and ephemeral. Gary Lee's guitar work is highly original, even brilliant in places, and the rhythm section grooves of my drum tracks and Van's bass lines make the band swing like a battleship in a hurricane.

Now in the 21st century, most albums are recorded to a click track (even I do this from time to time), or they are programmed with drum machines and laptop computers, which makes the music sound totally linear and extremely sterile—it utterly lacks *the swing*.

I tend to think that the greatest songs and greatest albums should be like human beings—a fluid, living, breathing entity. The body inhales and expands, and then it exhales and contracts, and so too should the feel of a song move like the wind in a human body, which is the soul of the song. This is also why when we hear a great band play, we feel it in a very different way. It reminds us of our earliest human origins, when we survived on natural, performed music, as we sat around the embers of the village fire.

That was the power of the Screaming Trees when we made *Sweet Oblivion* in the New York winter of 1992. We brought the fire from Seattle, magnified it in the manic swirl of New York City, and captured it all on magnetic tape, in real time, with swing and soul, and a fair bit of swagger. It's an album about love, hope, and the possibility of redemption, combined with a fearless abandon that says, "I will go for it all, right here and right now because I have nothing else to lose, and everything to gain."

The Screaming Trees flew to New York City as the underdogs of the Seattle music scene, but we came back as the new champions of songwriting.

And that is why *Sweet Oblivion* is still a classic album, three decades later.

FALLING REFRIGERATORS

For reasons that I cannot properly explain with logic, the Screaming Trees had a propensity for having cans and even bottles of beer thrown at us on stage, backstage, and at each other. Sometimes it was the idiot in the audience whose highest level of achievement in life was to see if he could hit a musician on stage with a bottle, a tennis ball, a coin, or sometimes even a rock. These are the lowest of humans, but these are the things a band had to contend with in the 1990s, and apparently, even today.

Back in 2019 when Mark was finalizing his memoir, he called to ask if I remembered certain events the same way he did, which of course we didn't. This led to a lot of laughing at our shared dementia, and that's when he reminded me that it was I who threw the first can of beer in his room at the Gramercy Park Hotel during the making of *Sweet Oblivion*. This unfortunately is true, however there is much more to the story, including the circumstances under which my beer chucking took place.

You see, when we went to New York to record *Sweet Oblivion*, the band was broke, but I was literally *broke ass broke*. This was because I had only been working for a few months at my construction job when I had to quit again in order to go to New York to make the album. After paying off my bills, I left Seattle with about $200 cash in my pocket and that was literally all the money I had in the world. I remember that I had to spend $100 on a leather jacket and a pair of boots at one of those cheap leather stores on 8th Street in Manhattan because I needed clothes for the photo shoot for the album cover. That left me with about $100 for food because our label had not given us any food money, so I literally had to survive on $3.00 a day, which was about two slices of pizza and a beer or a soda.

The whole situation was becoming absurd because here we were in New York, making the band's second major label album, yet we had no money to buy food. I lived on those $1.00 slices of pizza across the street from the hotel almost every day, and that was mostly what I ate for a month, except for the free coffee in the lobby of the hotel, and the occasional restaurant meal we would get from our A&R rep, Bob Pfeifer, which was once or twice a week at most.

The one thing the label did give us, however, were these booklets of car vouchers, which we could use to order a Lincoln Town Car to take us to and from the studio. The label had us working at the studio every day, arriving in a fancy car, but they never thought about getting us food. I guess it was all about appearances in New York.

Each band member had a booklet of these car vouchers, which Van, Lee, and I would ration to get to the studio, hours before Mark would arrive. Meanwhile, Mark was using up all his car vouchers riding around town and raising all kinds of hell, which he would later recount to us at the studio, much to our great amusement. Mark was a great storyteller, even back then, and after telling us a story from the night before, he would cut his vocal tracks on the music we had been working on that day. This work methodology seemed to work just fine—until Mark ran out of car vouchers.

Mark called my hotel room one evening after I had returned from the studio, and said that he really needed more car vouchers. I told him I only had a couple left and I was out of money, so I couldn't afford to take a taxi until we got paid, which is the eternal problem with bands on major labels. Somehow Mark sweet-talked me into taking my vouchers down to his room, which he promptly snatched out of my hands like a fiend, as soon as he opened the door. I was instantly infuriated by his rude behavior, and I used this as an opportunity to lecture him on the art of better manners towards his band mates, and that I, the newest member of the band, wasn't even getting money for food while I was recording on his band's album.

I didn't know Mark that well at the time, and I had really only been in the rehearsal room with him as we worked on the songs for the album. We had previously gotten along just fine, and we had a jovial, friendly manner between us. I was just as tall as Mark, and a little bit beefier, so I wasn't about to take any guff from this "lead singer." He responded to my lecture not with contrition or anger, but with two simple words, which I remember exactly:

"Tough titty."

This enraged me to the point of a total meltdown, to the degree that I screamed something unintelligible at the top of my lungs, and hurled my freshly opened can of Rolling Rock (the one can I could afford per day) as hard as I could at his head. It missed by a mile, hitting the wall behind him with a resounding, foaming thud.

This was a bad look for me because I had previously bragged to Mark about my baseball pitching abilities when I was in little league, a conversation that had been sparked by Mark's admission that he had been a quarterback for the Ellensburg High School football team, where he achieved a school record for the most interceptions in a season. Apparently, we were both failed athletes who had become musicians with burgeoning drinking problems.

With the realization that my beer can had missed by a huge margin, Mark started laughing hysterically and he jumped out of his chair and hugged me exuberantly, exclaiming, "You must have been raised by alcoholics too!"

This made me laugh and cry a little because it was true, I had been. And to be honest, I felt quite emotional during that period of time, because making a record like *Sweet Oblivion* was one of the most intense experiences of my life. We were under huge pressure to deliver, and we were broke at the same time. My explosion of anger dissipated and suddenly everything was fine between us, in fact, I think we became brothers in that moment because we understood certain things about each other. I learned that Mark, although he could be very selfish and self-absorbed at times, also had a keen sense of humor that could diffuse most situations. And Mark saw in me that, despite my propensity for flashes of rage, I was loyal to the band and I would get into actual street battles to protect the guys in the Trees, as some of these future stories will illustrate.

Another incident of beer projectiles also happened during the making of *Sweet Oblivion*, when we had the opportunity to play an opening set for the band, Dinosaur Jr., at the Roseland ballroom in Manhattan. The Roseland was an historic venue, where swing bands from the WWII era used to play, and now in the 1990s it was rock bands who roared within its sacred walls. The Trees played our opening set for Dino (as the hipsters called them), and we had a killer show because of all the rehearsing and recording that we had just been doing. After we toweled off the sweat, the four of us re-assembled on the side of the stage to watch Dino play their set.

As they took the stage, and for reasons unknown, Mark started to heckle the band. Being that they were old friends from the SST days, and that their bass player, Mike Johnson, was the guitarist in Mark's solo band, the heckling seemed more like good-natured ribbing—until it wasn't.

At some point, Mike Johnson had reached his limit, as he spun around on the heels of his trademark wing-tipped loafers, kicking an empty beer bottle towards our side of the stage. At this point, the spirit of David Beckham entered the game, as the bottle did a supernatural arc through the air, spinning and whistling like a UFO, as it curved towards the Trees. Suddenly, the bottle zeroed in on Mark, striking him exactly in the middle of his forehead, making that uniquely hollow, metallic thud that beer bottles on skulls make. Mark staggered backwards in disbelief, but he never went down—he kept his footing, albeit in a state of shock. Mike didn't miss a note on his bass either, and we were all flabbergasted at the ferocity and accuracy of his kick. The heckling ceased.

The following day, Mark sported an enormous goose egg on his forehead, which seemed to last for months, and it was still visible when we started the touring cycle for *Sweet Oblivion*.

It was near the end of that first US tour for *Sweet Oblivion* that my initial beer chucking karma came back to haunt me. It happened right after the Trees had played a truly magnificent show in Cincinnati, Ohio. The show itself went on for something close to three hours, and we played absolutely every song we could remember, plus three encores filled with cover songs by The Velvet Underground, Cream, the MC5, and Devo. The very last encore turned into a Q & A with Mark, where the audience would ask him questions, and he would answer in the most hilarious and good-natured way. I'd never seen this side of Mark, he was so completely comfortable with the audience, responding to them with some really great stories and one-liners.

After Mark's encore/comedy routine ended, we finally left the stage and went backstage to our dressing room. That's when Mark said something to Lee about the quality of his guitar sound—it was more shrill and piercing than usual. I said something about the overall stage sound being kind of bad, which I thought was a neutral comment that might diffuse the situation, but it had the opposite effect, as Lee became totally enraged. He suddenly hurled a full, unopened beer bottle at my head, which I instinctively ducked and barely missed, feeling it graze the back of my neck as it stuck, bottlenose first, into the sheetrock wall behind my head. It would have certainly knocked me unconscious or perhaps even killed me if it had hit me in the temple, and this infuriated Van, who roared like a bull elephant as he lunged at his brother Lee in a full frontal take down.

The brothers, each weighing in at over 300 pounds, began brawling as they alternately wrestled and punched at each other, destroying the entire backstage in the process. Deli trays were flung about, coolers with ice and beer were overturned, and I was caught in the middle of it all. At one point, the brothers collided against a massive 1950s industrial refrigerator, which toppled over, taking me down with it, and landing on top of me. I was now at the bottom of the dog pile, the fridge on top, with Van and Lee howling and brawling on the top of the fridge. I was crushed under their combined weight and could barely breathe—I was about to pass out.

Our tour manager finally broke up the fight, and I was able to extract myself from under the wreckage. It was only then that I saw Mark sitting in an armchair in the corner of the room, laughing so hard that he was doubled over and unable to breathe himself. That's when I knew the law of karma had returned on me.

So let me tell you, grandchildren: if you throw anything at anyone, you will most surely have a similar object thrown back at you, even if it's many years later.

And it might even include a large kitchen appliance.

THE VALIANT VS. THE TREE

When I returned to Seattle after recording *Sweet Oblivion*, I felt triumphant in a musical sense, but I also found myself homeless for the first time in my young, 24-year-old life. It was largely because I had given up my awesome warehouse loft in downtown Seattle, but I was also making the transition from being a full-time carpenter, to being a full-time musician in the Screaming Trees, a band that could barely afford to buy food for it's members, much less housing. As I described in a previous story, house-building and album-making are very parallel disciplines, in that both structures are built in layers upon a strong foundation. What makes each house and each album unique, is the care that the builders put into their creation.

I was now regretting my decision to give up my loft, where my first three bands had all rehearsed and written songs. I was under the impression that the Trees were going to immediately hit the road and start touring after making *Sweet Oblivion*, but that had been delayed by the album release date being pushed back to September. Instead, we were now looking at some scattered shows and short tours throughout the spring and summer.

I couldn't go back to the warehouse anyway, as it had been taken over by some very strange folks who were more interested in smoking pot all day, cutting holes in the roofs of their cars, and then filling them up with water from a garden hose so they could soak in their "hot tub cars." I witnessed this very bizarre activity the one day I went to visit an old roommate who was still living there—I certainly wasn't going back there now. I also decided that I didn't want to live downtown anymore—I had done that for almost five years. I wanted to find a quiet neighborhood, so I went hunting for a proper home with its own private bathroom, a luxury I didn't have in my old loft.

I was temporarily staying with a girlfriend who I had met in college, and we had been off and on since the Skin Yard days. At this point, it was time for the relationship to be permanently off because admittedly, it would be hard to date a musician who was ready to hit the road at a moment's notice. I was way more excited to leave Seattle than stay, so a relationship with me was probably not a good choice. She graciously allowed me to stay at her swanky Capital Hill condo until I found my own place, but the problem with Seattle apartments, even 30 years ago, was that they were extremely expensive, and almost as much as renting a house. Maybe I should find a roommate and just go for a house instead?

Van Conner and I had gotten along extremely well when we were roommates at the Gramercy Park Hotel, so I called him up to see if perhaps he might want to go in on a rental house with me. Hopefully it would have a basement too, as many Seattle houses did, and then we could practice as a rhythm section.

We ended up finding a great little house in the musician-friendly Green Lake neighborhood, where I liked to walk from time to time. That neighborhood is now one of the wealthiest in the city, but 30 years ago it was actually kind of run down, and full of musicians and creative types in general. After much hoop-jumping to prove that we could pay the rent, we got a year-long lease on the house, and we moved in with only the spartan furniture we had accumulated between the two of us—a single hand me down couch, a kitchen table with a couple of chairs, and an old TV set, which I inherited from my parents when they moved to Australia a couple years earlier.

This is how Van and I set up our musical home that we would occupy for the next couple years, just a block from the Latona Pub, where we ate cheap hot dogs and drank various kinds of micro-beers. That's also when Mark started coming over to visit us, I think because he liked the homey, neighborhood vibe that half of his band was creating.

People came and went from our house, and we had some very cool neighbors across the street, who were a group of female musicians. They were rocker girls, or more accurately, they were some of the first *Riot Grrrls* to come out of the northwest music scene. They would come over after their day jobs had finished to drink beer and smoke cigarettes with us, and we would talk about the music scene we were all cultivating.

The whole *Riot Grrrl* thing actually started in my hometown of Olympia, but it was fast becoming a nationwide phenomenon. The Riot Grrrls were smart, politically-active women, modern feminists really, who also loved the power of indie rock as a form of expression. The girls across the street from us were totally of this ethos and we liked them a lot, although it was always just a friendship between us, there was nothing romantic that ever transpired. We usually talked about new bands that were forming in Seattle and across the country, and what was happening around the world politically. It was a great time to be young and creative, and we realized that we were part of something that was becoming much bigger than any of us could have ever imagined.

Mark came over on one of those evenings in the spring of 1992, and he proceeded to hold court with the Riot Grrrls in our living room. I think he thought he might get lucky with one of them, which he didn't, but he continued to party with us throughout the evening, to the degree that he was certainly not capable of driving, and definitely shouldn't have attempted it. As he got up to leave, he started walking to our driveway where his 1962 Plymouth Valiant was parked, the same one Kurt Cobain had given him. I followed behind and insisted that he not drive, and that I would be happy to take him back to his apartment on Capital Hill. I actually loved driving around Seattle back then, it was so quick and easy, but Mark wasn't having any of it. He got into his Valiant and started it up, revving the engine exactly like the time he drove us to *The Lusty Lady*. Then he began backing out of the driveway.

The angle of his car was way off, to the degree that within a few seconds, he had managed to hook the right corner of the front bumper around the trunk of a tall cypress tree that lined the driveway. He had snagged the tree, fishhook style, and it wasn't going to budge.

By this time, I was screaming at Mark that he had to pull forward so that the bumper could unhook itself from the tree, but he wasn't having any of that logic either. Instead, he gunned the accelerator and roared the car in reverse, the tires spitting gravel in all directions. Suddenly, there was a terrible, metallic groan, as the chrome bumper wrenched itself from the frame, and the cypress tree swayed back and forth victoriously with the kinetic release of the destroyed bumper. The cypress wasn't going anywhere, and it had triumphed in the tug of war with the Valiant.

The right front fender was clearly indented from the trunk of the tree, and the bumper sagged downward with a crooked smile. It was barely connected to the frame by a single bolt on the opposite side, as it dragged along the ground like a dislocated jawbone from Detroit's golden age of dinosaur cars.

Mark was now in the street, the bumper scraping along the asphalt. Thank god no one was coming, much less a cop because he slammed it into drive and roared off into the night, the bumper emitting sparks of light from under the severely mutilated Valiant.

I think that was the moment when I saw something very different in Mark. He was someone who could be immensely talented and hilariously funny, yet there was also something very dark underneath it all, something very self-destructive. That darkness would grow as the years rolled on, but in that moment, I simply attributed it to Mark just being Mark.

We had been working together for about 6 months at that point, playing occasional shows and partying together in the truest sense of a brotherhood. It was a hugely creative and transformative period we had just experienced together, but I also began to see how alcohol could cause a man to destroy a perfectly preserved, vintage car.

It was an omen of things to come.

A GRAND ENTRANCE

It was now June of 1992, and the Trees were finally headed out on a proper tour of Europe. I quit my construction job for the last time, and off we went to play the summer rock festivals, as well as some club dates where the Trees would headline. This was a traditional strategy that many rock bands employed back then, right before they were about to release an album. The idea was to play to the biggest audiences possible (at the festivals), do as much press as possible to get a buzz going about your forthcoming album, and then do several club shows to get the band tight, and then hit the ground running when your album is released.

The Trees didn't have a tour bus at the time, nor could we have afforded one. We still didn't have a real budget to support our touring, most of which was done on the tiniest shoestring you can imagine. All we had was a small equipment van that had previously been a British milk delivery truck—the "milk truck" as we called it, and we had hired two crew guys for minimum wage. One of them was another Ellensburg alum, the Trees longtime tour manager, Rod Doak, and the other was a guitar tech named Jim Vincent, who would later go on to be Kurt Cobain's personal guitar tech. For this tour, however, both crewman were in charge of the milk truck and our equipment.

We also had Kim White with us, who was now managing the Trees while she juggled her executive duties at Geffen Records. Kim had used her accumulated vacation time to oversee this European tour, and set up the release of *Sweet Oblivion*. She also had a credit card, something none of us had enough credit to get, and she had rented a very nice Peugeot sedan for the band to ride in. Kim and I traded off driving duties since I had been the drummer/driver in Skin Yard and I loved driving. Why not continue this tradition in the Trees?

The Peugeot seating configuration usually consisted of me in the driver seat, Kim in the passenger seat, and the Conner brothers in the rear seats. Mark decided that he would rather sleep on a mattress that had been placed on top of the gear in the back of the milk truck, with the two crewmen in the cab, and this is how we caravaned from gig to gig across Europe.

We had just played a great, bombastic show in Vienna, Austria, and were on our way to Trieste, Italy the next day. This required driving through Slovenia, a brand new country that had recently separated itself from the former Yugoslav republic. I had actually played in the Slovenian capitol of Ljubljana with Skin Yard the previous year, and it was perhaps the best show on our entire 1991 European tour. During the week that Skin Yard played and stayed in Ljubljana, we made friends with several college students who showed us all around the city, and who demonstrated the warmth and kindness of the Slovenian people. That will become an important part of this story in a moment.

We had left Vienna early in the morning because of the distance to Trieste, a beautiful city in the northeastern corner of Italy on the Adriatic Sea. The route took us through Slovenian and Italian customs along the way, and this could take a considerable amount of time, depending on the mood of the customs officials on any given day. Fortunately, the Slovenian customs was a breeze, they waved us straight through with the friendliness I remembered from the Skin Yard tour, but at the Italian border, the notoriously difficult border guards pulled us over for an inspection.

Now, the Italian border guards back then were notorious for their corruption, including creating drama as an excuse to do elaborate searches. There is even a famous case where the guards made a certain band set up their equipment and play songs to prove to the guards that they were actually a band. Thus, we expected the worst as we pulled into the search area.

There was nothing to be found on us or in the car, as we never carried drugs or any other kind of illegal substance across borders, however, the guards became suspicious of Van's generic vitamin pills. Any reasonable person could tell they were drugstore-grade vitamins, but these were Italian border guards where reasonableness is not in their vocabulary. After two hours of waiting for their narcotics tester to arrive with a chemical kit to test the mysterious pills, they ultimately decided that they had harassed us long enough and let us go. On to Trieste we went, hoping that our equipment truck would make it through without any problems.

Upon arriving at the venue in Trieste, we were happy to find that our show was to be held inside a castle that had been remodeled for live concerts. Its interior courtyard had been replaced with a huge central lawn, with a stage at one end, and seating or standing on the central lawn for the audience. It was a beautiful place to play a show, and it couldn't get any more *Spinal Tap* than to play inside a castle. The Trees were excited, especially on this warm, sunny evening.

We had arrived in the early afternoon, far ahead of the equipment truck, so we had enough time to walk around the area, have a dignified lunch, and we came back with plenty of time for our sound check. Our crew was setting up the stage when we returned, but Mark wasn't with them—he hadn't ridden in the milk truck after all.

The rest of us thought Mark had ridden in the back of the truck as per his usual custom, because he liked to sleep on the mattress on top of the gear after partying all night after the shows. That's when one of the crewman said that Mark had stayed behind in Vienna to party with some local fans, under the premise that they would give him a ride to Trieste the following day.

When it came time to do the sound check, the Conner brothers and I played a few songs with each of us singing the lead vocals. Lee sang most of the songs since he did most of the back up vocals, but I sang occasionally too, and the three of us had developed a great harmonic balance between our vocals. Sometimes we all had to sing during an encore, especially if Mark left the stage early and we had to pull out several of the many cover songs we could play. But here in Trieste, there was also another issue developing.

You see, back in the 1990s, if you played a show in Italy, the promoters were almost always connected to the mafia in some way. They owned most of the nightclubs and live venues, and likely the drug and alcohol sales too. They had a pattern of making the bands feel more like hired restaurant employees than artists, and we were not getting off to a good start here in Trieste. The Trees even had a bomb threat made on their previous tour of Italy, right before I joined the band, because they had played a show with a promoter who was not connected to the right mob family. These were simple-minded, thuggish goons, they were not smart, and they were not wise. They were more akin to gorillas in Armani suits.

At our show in Trieste, these goons started making veiled threats, saying that we would have to play without Mark or else there would be trouble. Well, the Trees each stood at over 6'3" and we had a combined weight of well over 1,000 pounds between us, so even with Mark missing there were still three of us, plus our two crew guys—and Kim, who was much tougher than her outward beauty would imply. These mafia clowns were puny by comparison and we were not intimidated, but we were concerned about the whereabouts of Mark—what had happened to him? At the same time, we wanted to play our show for the large audience of excited fans who had gathered on the immense lawn in front of us because that's who we were playing for.

As the time ticked by, our start time came and went, and we were getting ready to take the stage as a trio without Mark when a commotion began to happen near the back entrance behind the stage. It was Mark, busting through security, straddled on the back of a moped. Let me reiterate this for clarity—it was Mark was on a moped. Not a scooter or a motorcycle, but a moped.

You can't begin to imagine the absurdity of this, it was a totally ridiculous scene that was completely incongruous with the image we all had of Mark, yet it was totally him at the same time. There he was, his long red hair whipping up behind him, still drunk and laughing all the way to the back of the stage, as the moped dramatically pulled up behind my drum riser. And who do you think was at the helm of that moped? None other than the long-haired, bearded college student I had befriended and hung out with in Slovenia a year earlier on that Skin Yard tour. He had randomly found Mark drinking in a bar on the way to the show and offered to give him a ride to the castle.

We hit the stage immediately and the show went off without a hitch, in fact, it was one of our best shows of the tour and the audience loved it. The gangster-goons stayed out of our way, I guess they were happy with their financial haul, and we ended our set at exactly the time agreed upon in our performance contract. We decided to end the night early and get a good night's sleep in our hotel rooms, and even Mark agreed to this.

The next day we had a very long, 7-hour drive to Rome, a drive that most certainly could not be done on a moped.

BETWEEN THE WHEELS

Most drives on a European tour are within a 3-4 hour range at most, and in that amount of time, you can easily drive across the entirety of some of the smaller countries. You can see how the Germans rolled across Europe so quickly at the beginning of World War II—most of the countries are only a few hundred miles across. The problems arise when you get on one of the German Autobahns, their freeway system, which has no speed limit and can send you racing off in the wrong direction if you don't know exactly where you are going. Taking into account that this was in 1992, about 20 years before anyone had GPS on their phones, when we used actual paper maps, and we had to watch the road signs carefully.

Such was the case on one of our morning drives across Germany, when I got on the Autobahn going to what I thought was Frankfurt. Once we were on the Autobahn, I took advantage of its no speed limit, combined with the fact that the Peugeot could easily go 100 mph without the slightest speed wobble. In a conversation I had with Gary Lee, he remembered that I was actually going about 130 mph for about an hour and half. That's when we started seeing signs for a totally different German city that was in the opposite direction of where we wanted to go. When I finally realized my mistake, I had driven about 200 miles in the wrong direction, which added 400 miles just to get us back to where we started. We barely made it to the gig that night.

On the morning after the Trieste show, we faced a looming 7-hour drive to Rome, and I was definitely not going to make the same mistake I had made on the German Autobahn. We were excited to play in Rome, and we made sure Mark was safely inside the back of the milk truck, which was now being driven by our newest and third crew hire, Martin Feveyear. Martin was a British sound man fleeing a terrible divorce, as well as the claustrophobic town of Ipswich. He had become a road refugee like the rest of us, so he fit right in as a driver, which eventually led to him becoming our front of house sound man.

We had to get a very early start in order to make it in time for the sound check in Rome, so I took the wheel of the Peugeot with the determination to get us there on time, with Kim as navigator in the passenger seat, and the Conner brothers in the back seat. The milk truck was already ahead of us, so they could get the gear set up on time.

The main Italian freeways are very much like the German Autobahns, in that there really isn't a speed limit. It's normal for most vehicles to be driving about 100 mph, but its also quite common to see a supercar like a Ferrari or a Lamborghini fly by at a much faster speed, closer to 150 mph—they pass you like you're standing still. I was driving in the 100 mph range because although the Peugeot was a well-engineered sedan, I wanted to play it safe and follow the slow but steady method. I gauged our speed by the distance we had to cover, and everything seemed on target.

The weather was fairly nice as I remember, it was summer in Europe after all, but a couple hours into the drive, I noticed some thunderheads forming in the distance—the summer monsoons. I could see rain coming down far away, a cloudburst on the horizon that had opened up in the sky, but it was still totally dry where we were. Very quickly, however, the road started to get wet with rain, and soon it was thoroughly soaked from a heavy downpour that was suddenly surrounding us. It was creating huge puddles of standing water on the freeway and I knew I had to slow down because of the dreaded hydroplane effect, as well as the accumulation of all the motor oil that soaks into every highway, making the roads slick and deadly.

No need to worry about an oil slick, however, because we were suddenly hydroplaning on a massive lake of standing water—going 100 mph.

I had been driving in the inside, fast lane, as there was a string of large semi-trucks in the slower, right lane that I wanted to pass. However, the trucks were also driving incredibly fast, dangerously so, and they too had hit the standing water. The truck to our right hydroplaned at the same time we did.

I can't explain exactly what happened next, and I have no idea what was going through the mind of the truck driver, but what happened to us was the closest I had ever come to death up to that point in my life.

As the Peugeot began to hydroplane, I followed my instincts to keep the steering wheel absolutely straight, making no sharp turns or sudden movements. It was like staring down a bear, which I think is the same advice. The car was starting to float to the right, directly underneath the truck's trailer, and right in between its front and rear axles.

As we continued to hydroplane under the truck's trailer, I kept the speed matched with the truck so that we stayed between the wheels. At the worst point, we drifted exactly halfway under the trailer, with the right half of the Peugeot under the trailer, and the left half still in our lane, exactly between the front and rear axles.

Everyone in the car screamed, and I mean they *screamed*, except for me—I was dead silent because I had to concentrate on driving. And when I say the band screamed, I mean they screamed like Steve Martin and John Candy in the movie, *Planes, Trains and Automobiles (1987)*, when the two characters drive between two oncoming semi-trucks, with sparks flying off the side of their car, and Steve Martin looks at John Candy who turns into a laughing devil in a costume, and I think that's exactly how my passengers saw me.

I knew in that instant that this was a life or death situation, and I knew that I could not move the wheel suddenly, else we would spin out of control and go underneath the wheels of the truck. I had to keep the Peugeot exactly the same speed as the truck, while slowly easing the steering wheel to the left, and out from under the trailer bed. I instinctively tilted my head to the left, which made the wheel turn slightly in that direction, as we inched our way back into our lane and on to dry pavement again. The truck driver continued as if nothing had happened, and perhaps he didn't even know the drama unfolding under his trailer. But I have a feeling he did.

For the remaining few hours of the drive to Rome, everyone in the car stayed completely and utterly silent. I think they were contemplating their lives. Van was probably thinking about his last meal, Lee was probably thinking about the meal he was going to eat when we finally arrived in Rome, and Kim was probably worrying about her ballooning credit card bill, which we kept adding to. I was thinking about a newspaper story about a band killed on the way to their show in Rome, killed by their drummer.

When we finally arrived in Rome that evening, we found to our delight that the venue was directly opposite the Vatican—you could see it from the entrance to the theater. We were surprised that a rock show could even happen with such close proximity to the Holy See of Christendom, then again, the mafia connection. It was a huge show for us too—the Romans really turned out for the Trees, as we played a powerful show in a gorgeous theater for an ecstatic audience. Anyone who has ever toured Europe will tell you that the best audiences are in Italy, they just love the rock & roll.

After doing a couple encores, we started to leave the stage and I had a bottle of water in my hands. For some subconscious reason, I felt compelled to bless the audience by throwing holy water at them in the shape of a cross. I'd never done anything like that before or since because I was never a Catholic or much of a Christian for that matter, but somehow I felt the urge to do it there, right next to the Vatican. I was waiting for lighting to strike me, but I had felt some higher power out there on the Italian motorway and I wanted to pass that along to the audience, however strange that might seem.

I once heard a guy tell me, "I love Jesus like I love Elvis—I love the men and their example, it's the cults I can't stand." I suppose I feel the same way.

After the Rome show and the near death experience on the freeway, Kim decided that she needed a break from the touring life. Kim had Italian heritage so we dropped her off in Rimini on the way back north, and that's when she said to me, "I just need to be with my people for a while."

We totally understood, the Trees were a handful, and we left her at a beautiful sidewalk café, where she immediately ordered a large glass of red wine, her dark sunglasses holding back the tears.

Kim and her credit card would be back with the Trees a week later, she caught a train and met up with us in Denmark, just in time for some real festival fun.

ROCKSLIDE AT ROSKILDE

That first European tour with the Screaming Trees in the summer of 1992 might have been my favorite of all the tours I would do with the band in the coming decade. It had everything a great tour should have: shows that were mostly sold out, extremely beautiful venues, incredible late night dinners in ancient cities, marvelous high speed driving on perfect Autobahn superhighways, and we played two huge festivals with our good friends, Nirvana. Their band was blowing up around the world like a nuclear event, which musically is exactly what it was. It was incredible to witness it in real time, and to be able to congratulate them personally.

I even broke my left ankle on the very last night of the tour, after an amazing dinner in Paris where we drank a lot of wine. We had been walking around the Cemetery Montmartre after dinner, looking at the graves of artists, poets, and composers when we realized that the giant 10-foot gates where we entered had been locked behind us. We had to climb over the top of the enormous stone walls in order to get back to our hotel, and that is when I slipped and fell, shattering my ankle and lower leg on the cobblestones below.

I still have a limp from that fall, which is a permanent memory of the tour, and how alcohol would become my nemesis. Still, whenever I feel the stiffness in my leg, I am reminded of that tour with the Trees in the summer of 1992. So many things had happened in that short year, but it also seemed like a lifetime had unfolded in the same amount of time.

By July of 1992, advance CDs for *Sweet Oblivion* were being sent out to media outlets around the world, and it was starting to create a real stir in the same way that Nirvana's and Pearl Jam's breakthrough albums had done in the preceding year. The Trees shows were almost always sold out, and we played a mixture of songs from *Sweet Oblivion*, as well as the best songs from the Trees older albums from the SST and Sub Pop catalog. The audiences were devouring everything we played, and our sound was becoming tighter and more ferocious every night.

To put this in context, a rock show in the US that might only draw 300 people would draw closer to 1,000 people in Europe. Shows in Europe were literally three to four times bigger than anything in the US, and I think this is because Europeans tend to be hipper and more embracing of new music—such has been my experience over the decades.

Unlike the US, where the promoters often treated our bands with disdain because they actually had to work to promote the shows, the European promoters were very excited to have American bands playing in their clubs, and they welcomed us as honored guests. In doing so, Europe made the American bands feel much more appreciated and very motivated to tour over there, and the European audiences reflected that excitement.

Even our crew guys seemed to be enjoying themselves, which is not always the case working on a fast-paced, semi-chaotic tour like ours was. I also think that being the newest member of the Trees, I had something to do with a different energy the band was experiencing. New band members always change the chemistry of a group, sometimes for the better, sometimes for the worse. It was obvious that I was a positive force in the band, in that I was young, I was excited about our great album, and I never did drugs. I was also full of creative energy, but this could sometimes flip and become a kind of hot-tempered arrogance when I would lose my patience and fire off withering verbal assaults faster than a Buddy Rich single stroke roll. I suppose my physical size protected me from the backlash I might have received otherwise, because I looked more like a linebacker than a drummer, and I was in the best physical shape of my life. But as they say, the bigger they are, the harder they fall, as was the case with my permanently destroyed left ankle.

I also developed what I thought was a legitimate strategy for drinking responsibly. Mine was built around driving because I had driven the Skin Yard van so much on those North American tours, that I would never consider having a drink after a show if I had to drive the van. I would drink coffee instead, getting jacked up on the upper of caffeine, rather than the downer of alcohol, and I'd drive the van into the sunrise with no problem at all. If someone else was driving, I would use the opportunity to drink after the show, and at any bar or party that we happened to stop at along the way. As the years wore on, this would become a terrible pattern for me because I started to drink out of boredom, especially once we had a tour bus, when riding on a bus can be one of the most boring things a musician has to endure.

On this first European tour, one of the biggest shows we played was at the famous Roskilde Festival in Denmark, and once again, it was alcohol that would be our undoing.

Every band that was doing anything important in music was playing at the Roskilde Festival that summer: Nirvana, Pearl Jam, Blur, Helmet, David Byrne, Mind Funk, Megadeth, Primal Scream, Crowded House, Phish, Television, The Pogues…the list of the most happening bands in the world were there. Thus, it was a huge honor that Nirvana, and specifically Kurt Cobain, had asked the Screaming Trees to play as their opener right before Nirvana headlined the main stage.

By the time we arrived at the gigantic festival grounds just west of Copenhagen, the Trees had become a well-tuned rock & roll machine. Our live shows had more than a few streaks of wildness, which would explode on stage and either launch us into an epic musical performance, or cause the band to swing wildly off kilter. Either scenario seemed possible because with the Trees, consistency was not our strongest point—but unpredictable brilliance was. Even when the shows leaned toward the chaotic, people loved it, and when alcohol was involved, the emphasis was on the unpredictable, which was magnified tenfold.

As we drove to the backstage area in our ridiculous milk truck, Peugeot caravan, we began to see the enormity of the festival. At least 100,000 people were out there in the hot, dusty field that went as far as the eye could see. We were so far north that the sun only briefly dipped below the horizon at 4am, before rising again an hour later—it was the land of the midnight sun.

We parked backstage and tracked down our dressing room, which we found to be stocked with a short supply of beer (apparently quite expensive in Scandinavia), but a huge overabundance of the absolutely horrific German beverage that tastes like cough syrup—Jägermeister. They must have been doing some kind of promotion at the festival because there were Jägermeister signs everywhere and we had several full size bottles of the sewage-colored libation in our dressing room. I imagine the strategy was to limit the beer supply and stock up every band's dressing room with Jägermeister, in the hopes that the musicians would actually drink the horror. The strategy must have worked because drink it they did, and Jägermeister seemed to become the most popular alcohol in the world that year, until it finally waned into obscurity. For some unholy reason, Mark acquired a real taste for it, replacing his usual gin and tonics with the black goo, as he started working his way through the various bottles in our dressing room.

I never drank alcohol before a show, but even I had a shot of it, along with whiskey and a beer chaser, my usual combination. Perhaps it was because Roskilde was my first big festival ever and I was feeling a bit nervous to be opening for Nirvana, but for whatever reason, I did not take the stage in my best form, nor did the other Trees.

Our day to play was Friday, June 26th, 1992, and as we had been told, Nirvana was supposed to be headlining that night, with the Trees playing an opening set right before. At the last minute, however, Kurt Cobain decided that Nirvana should play before the Trees, but no reason was given for his change, so Nirvana got bumped to the earlier slot playing right before the Trees. Maybe it was Kurt's sly way of saying to the world: check out the Screaming Trees, Nirvana should be opening for them. Nirvana had opened for the Trees in 1990, and Kurt looked up to Mark, often seeking out his advice. Or maybe Kurt just wanted to go back to his hotel and get an early night's sleep, which anyone who has ever been on tour knows is a golden opportunity. None of us really knew Kurt's reason, but Nirvana was now opening for the Screaming Trees at the Roskilde Festival in the summer of 1992.

I have to re-emphasize that at this time in history, Nirvana was blowing up so fast you couldn't keep track of their ascent. By the time a radio or sales chart had been released to the public, Nirvana had already surpassed it. Their second album, *Nevermind* (1991)was becoming the most popular album in the world, knocking Michael Jackson out of the #1 spot on the Billboard sales chart, and their global popularity was akin to that of The Beatles or Led Zeppelin when those bands took over the world. Suddenly Nirvana was next in line to the throne as the biggest band in the world on just their second album.

Nirvana played a magnificent show that night at Roskilde, but suffice it to say that playing *after* Nirvana is about the worst situation a band could find itself in. It's a bit like playing after the Super Bowl, when the groundskeepers are sweeping up the mess. That's what the festival grounds looked like, because when Nirvana played that night, it was estimated that over 100,000 people were in the audience. I watched from the side of the stage and saw a sea of humanity totally enraptured by their music. When they finished their set an hour later, the Trees finally took the stage and the audience shrunk to half that number, but it was still close to 50,000 people, by far the largest audience we had ever played to.

Krist Novoselic, bassist for Nirvana, stood on the side of the stage to watch the Trees as we launched into our set with a brand new song, "Shadow Of The Season," which was the opening track to *Sweet Oblivion*. It was a great song to start our show, and we continued to play a mixture of the best of the old Trees songs, as well as some of our new ones, which of course no one in the audience had heard yet. Still, the audience loved the Trees, and they roared with enthusiasm after we finished every song.

As we played on, I pummeled the crap out of my drums because, having once played a show with Skin Yard opening for Nirvana in Vienna, Austria the previous year, I wasn't about to be upstaged by Dave Grohl—I had to at least meet the same ferocious energy. In fact, I had been touring with Skin Yard in 1990 when we met up with Kurt Cobain and Krist Novoselic at a club in San Francisco called the I-Beam, up on Haight Street. Kurt and Krist had invited us to come watch Dave Grohl play with his old punk band, Scream. I was standing next to the extremely tall Krist as we watched Dave's incredible drumming, and I yelled upwards into his ear, "Krist, you better get that guy in your band before someone else does." Krist replied, dryly, "Yeah, I think that's exactly what were going to do."

Here we were again, only two years later, and I was swinging as hard as I could to propel the Trees and the 50,000 audience members into unison. Mark seemed to be doing great with his singing, but then I noticed he was starting to stagger around the stage unevenly, a lot more than his usual swagger—the Jägermeister was starting to kick in. Then Mark suddenly snapped his mic stand in half, something he would do from time to time as a stage move, where he would break the stand right at the joint where the base meets the boom. That's when I knew things were starting to go sideways, but we were still rocking pretty good, and the huge audience seemed to be enjoying Mark's antics.

We had been playing for close to 40 minutes, so we were nearing the end of our set—at festivals, most bands play somewhere between 45 minutes to an hour, depending on their time slot. We started playing our last song, "Change Has Come", one of the Trees best songs from their 1989 Sub Pop EP of the same name. Mark's broken mic stand had now been replaced with a new one by guitar tech, Jim Vincent, but Mark's stumbling on stage was getting much worse. He was no longer in his usual stoic position behind the mic stand, with the two brothers bookending the stage. Instead, Mark had taken refuge, sitting in front of my bass drum on the drum riser.

It was becoming apparent that Mark was really quite wasted, and that's when Lee and Van sat down on either side of him, perhaps to give him support. All three of them were now sitting in front of my drums on the drum riser, and I thought it was very strange, but from my view behind the kit, they looked like a band of brothers gathering their energy for the final assault. Mark was yelling something into their ears as they sat side by side—what was going to happen?

Shortly after this gathering on the drum riser, Mark stood up, walked back to the mic stand, and suddenly threw it into the audience, after which he tried repeatedly to push a very large monitor off the front of the stage. This was a dangerous move because of the height of the stage, and because of the camera operators who were standing directly below, filming the show for Danish television. That's when the stage security guards and a couple stagehands started to come out from the wings to try and stop Mark. He fended them off with absurd, comical boxing stances that seemed more like Jerry Lewis' boxing movie than anything serious, but the stagehands, not wanting to actively fight a singer who was still performing on stage, backed away. That's when Mark finally succeeded in toppling the huge monitor off the front of the stage, which landed on top of the extremely expensive TV camera below. The monitor narrowly missed the cameraman and would have seriously wounded, if not killed him, if it had fallen directly on him.

The security guards rushed back out on stage and at that point, *it was on.* That's when Lee began swinging his Les Paul wildly by the headstock, smashing it on the stage like a crazed Berserker wielding his battle axe. Something suddenly kicked into me a well—perhaps it was the Jägermeister I had drunk earlier, because at that point I knew the show was over and we were way out in the weeds. I thought to myself, "Fuck it, I'll destroy this crappy rental drum set too."

I began throwing and kicking my drums off the riser, jumping down on to the main stage as I proceeded to smash up my cymbal stands with the same battle axe technique that Lee had done with his guitar, the cymbals still attached. I then exited stage right, as Mark continued to scuffle with the stage security until he finally gave the "hands up, I surrender", as he was escorted off stage left. For some odd reason, however, the security guards allowed Mark to go back out on stage and wave triumphantly to the crowd, like the court magician who had just completed his astonishing show.

At this point, all four us were now backstage and headed back to our dressing room, including an awestruck Mike McCready of Pearl Jam, who had played earlier that day. I didn't know it at the time, but Mike had been sitting behind my drum riser as I played the show, and he told me later that this was his favorite place to watch when the Trees were playing, so that he could feel the thunder of the drums. Mike was quite drunk too, because he had also been taken over by the spirit of Jägermeister, encouraged by Mark earlier in the day.

I was about to enter our dressing room, but I stopped at the threshold when I saw that Mark was in the process of completely destroying it. He was like Keith Moon smashing up a hotel room, and no one dared to go in there when Mark was in a fury. I headed over to the catering area to have some dinner because, you know, smashing up a drum set in front of 50,000 people makes a guy kind of hungry.

Our promoter for Roskilde was a gentleman named Mads, who I had met on that Skin Yard tour the previous year when he promoted our show in Copenhagen. Mads followed me into the catering area and I could tell immediately that he was extremely angry and upset about the carnage the Trees had caused on stage, specifically, the very expensive TV camera that Mark had just destroyed. Mads told me that we wouldn't be getting paid for the show because the TV camera cost about $100,000, and that was way more than the $10,000 guarantee that the Trees were supposed to be paid.

Then after a few moments of silent reflection Mads added, with a subtle grin:

"That was the greatest show I've seen since The Who played the Isle of Wight in 1970."

The Trees were never invited to play the Roskilde Festival ever again.

A BRAWL IN ASBURY PARK

It was now mid-September of 1992, and the Trees had just returned from a quick trip to England where we played the Reading Festival, and this time we actually opening for Nirvana. The day's line up had been personally cultivated by Kurt Cobain, where he hand-picked his favorite bands to play the show: The Melvins, Screaming Trees, Pavement, L7, Teenage Fanclub, Mudhoney, and Nick Cave and the Bad Seeds were the artists who performed until Nirvana took the stage and played one of the greatest concerts of their short but blinding career. I stood on the side of the stage by the monitor desk and watched the greatest live band on Earth, playing at the peak of their powers. That was a truly magnificent day, one for the history books as they say. Now it was time for the Trees to hit the road, as *Sweet Oblivion* had just been released.

We were starting to play headline shows in the largest clubs along the east coast, and on this particular night, we found ourselves in Asbury Park, New Jersey. Everyone involved in American music knows that Bruce Springsteen made his bones in this little seaside town, where he played multiple gigs at a club called *The Stone Pony*. That club is still going to this day, and it was on the following night that the Trees were to play this storied venue.

Our song, "Nearly Lost You," was a veritable radio hit, and our show at the Stone Pony was the night before we were going to be the musical guests on *Late Night With David Letterman*, which was the biggest TV show a band could play besides *Saturday Night Live*. The Trees were in a festive mood when we arrived in Asbury Park a day early, checking into our hotel, which was a short walking distance from *The Stone Pony*. We decided to head down to the club for dinner and drinks on our night off, as the promoter had offered this as a sign of generosity for our sold out show. There really wasn't much else to do that in that small town, so dinner and drinks on our night off seemed perfect.

I want to set up this story by saying that touring on the east coast is a much different scenario than touring on the west coast, largely because the cities on the eastern seaboard are geographically denser and much closer. It only takes a few hours to drive across New England, and it's only a 4-hour drive between Boston and New York City. By contrast, it takes about 12 hours to drive from Seattle to the next major city to the south, San Francisco.

The east coast is culturally different too, in more ways than a simple paragraph can explain. The east has less space for people and they guard their territory more zealously than the spacious west does. Being from the west we could feel it because the Trees were generally pretty laid back and not easily riled up, and this is partly why things went sideways for us on that particular night in Asbury Park. It was a territorial dispute that didn't make sense to us.

We had just ordered dinner and we were having a round of drinks, and we were really just kicking back and enjoying a night off in a mild-mannered way, in our corner of the bar. I wasn't even close to being drunk, as Van and I ate our steak and baked potatoes, sipping on whiskey and beer. Mark was drinking his usual gin and tonics and he seemed totally normal too, but then he got up and started walking towards the front door, gin and tonic in hand. I wondered where he was going, especially with his dinner left behind—maybe he recognized a friend who was coming to meet him, or maybe he was headed outside for a smoke. It could have been any number of reasons, however he just kept walking, straight out the front door, drink in hand, which I thought was a bit odd. I got up and followed to see if everything was OK.

What happened next is somewhat of a blur, yet I can still remember the general sequence of events as they unfolded. I definitely did not take my beer with me because I left it next to my dinner and I was open-handed as I approached the front door, walking out across the threshold into the crisp night air. I immediately saw two thugs assaulting Mark on the steps of the club, and I started to jump in to assist him, but was myself attacked by two more of these goons on the top of the stairs.

They were trying to hold my arms down and prevent me from fighting back, but I managed to struggle free, and that's when I started to feel the blows raining down. I felt no pain really, as one usually doesn't with the flood of adrenaline, and I landed a few punches myself, one across the jaw of one of my assailants. I heard his jaw crack, right as I lost my footing and tumbled down the stairs in a backwards somersault, rolling onto my feet as I landed at the bottom of the stairs onto the sidewalk.

At this point, Mark was free from his attackers and at the bottom of the stairs too, and he and I were literally standing back-to-back on the sidewalk, fists up and ready for another round with our random and extremely violent assailants. Who they were I had no idea, nor why they attacked us in the first place. A minute earlier, I had been eating a steak and drinking a cold beer. Was this an ambush, maybe some kind of gangland initiation ritual that we were totally unaware of?

There appeared to be more of them now too, perhaps as many as eight, emerging from the shadows and converging at the top of the stairs and around us. They appeared to be poised to attack as a group, and they had the high ground on us.

I screamed something to the effect of, "Come on down you chicken shit motherfuckers!" my courage fueled from years of Kung Fu with a Chinese master in Seattle that had started in the mid 1980s. I also had a shot whiskey in my belly, which is a kind of liquid courage. I was foolishly confident, much more than I should have been under the circumstances.

The Asbury Park goons stood at the top of the stairs glaring down at us, but Mark and I were both very tall and quite burly, and we were obviously ready to throw down and deliver some pain if another attack happened. For whatever reason, they did not attack, and the one whose jaw I had cracked on the stairs stood holding the side of his face with one hand. I think they knew that although they had gotten the surprise jump on us, it wouldn't be so easy the next time. And even though Mark and I were outnumbered, we were clearly not inexperienced in fighting. After a few tense moments, the goons sauntered sideways off the stairs and disappeared into the night like the cowards that they were.

When I asked Mark why they had jumped him in the first place, he said he had no idea—he said he walked outside with his drink and was immediately jumped, they had just come out of nowhere.

Up to that point, I had felt no pain and was only now starting to feel a strange sensation in my left shoulder, like a swelling or a tightness. I reached up with my right hand and could feel a lump growing where my collarbone met the shoulder. I could still move my shoulder, but it hurt and something was definitely off. At this point our tour manager, Rod Doak, emerged from the club and insisted that we walk straight back to our hotel in a group for safety reasons. He wanted to get us off the street in case the goons came back in larger numbers, which is what these cowards might do. We walked back to our hotel and I went straight to my room to look at my shoulder in the bathroom mirror, and as I removed my black T-shirt, I could see that something was very bad. I called Rod to my room to have a look, "Man, that's a really serious injury. It's either broken or dislocated, so we have to go to the emergency room right now."

Off we went to the Asbury Park ER, and after some X-rays and a consultation from the attending physician, he determined that it wasn't broken, but that it had been separated, probably when I rolled down the stairs backwards at the beginning of the fight. I would need to wear a sling to allow the shoulder to pull itself back into alignment, which it would do over the course of the next several days. A couple shows might need to be canceled in the interim, but within a week I should be able to play again, albeit with some painkillers to get me through the first few shows.

As it turned out, David Letterman's music director, Paul Shaffer, didn't want me to play on the TV show after all, because he had already booked a guest drummer named Steve Ferrone, who later played with Tom Petty. Paul wanted Steve to play with the Trees instead of me, and although Steve was a fantastic drummer, he didn't really get my drum parts correct for the song they chose, which was the obvious hit, "Nearly Lost You." Still, it was a pretty solid performance from the other three Trees, as they played along with Steve and Paul, and the late night band. Mark was sporting a real shiner under his left eye, a souvenir from the fight the night before, but that only added to the mystique of the brawling Screaming Trees.

As I watched the show from the green room backstage, my arm in a sling, I felt a mixture of sadness that I wasn't up there playing the drums, but also pride in seeing the Trees making their debut on a huge TV show that millions would watch. As it neared the end of the episode, Dave

Letterman himself invited all four of us out onto the stage to sample an Oktoberfest buffet that had been used as some kind of stage prop for the show. It was a very large spread of food, and as we stood next to Dave, he joked to the audience, "This is just a snack for the Screaming Trees."

All four of us began to sample the food as the closing credits rolled across the screen, and all was fine until Mark threw some food at Lee and our appearance on national television devolved into a minor food fight, which culminated in Van placing a hollow pumpkin on Lee's head. Dave Letterman seemed annoyed with the turn of events and scowled with disdain, and all of this can still be viewed on the ubiquitous YouTube.

The Trees were never invited to play on Dave Letterman's show again.

GOLDEN GLOVES

The fight at The Stone Pony in Asbury Park only added to the tough guy mystique of the Screaming Trees, and it would not be the last time we would be involved in scuffles and fisticuffs. In fact, I was amazed at the frequency in which they started to happen, because up until that point, the only fights I had ever been involved with was the handful of times I fought the neighborhood bully, but that was when I was 13 years old. Aside from some serious sparring at the Kung Fu dojo in Seattle, and then the Asbury Park incident, those were the only real fights I had ever been in. Yet here I was at the age of 25, with goons in nightclubs and on the streets actively looking for a scrape with the Screaming Trees.

During our first US tour for *Sweet Oblivion*, we had played quite a number of shows in the Deep South, with several shows in Florida in particular. The South was always good to the Trees, it was a great place to play rock & roll because some of the greatest musical artists in American history came from there—the Allman Brothers (Georgia), Tom Petty (Florida), not to mention Elvis (Mississippi), Johnny Cash (Arkansas), and all the great blues and soul singers from the Mississippi Delta who started it all. The Trees loved and were heavily influenced by all of that music, we revered it, and in return, the South loved the Trees right back.

This southern magnetism that we had cultivated led to several shows in Florida that were promoted by a company called Cellar Door, and for the most part, they did a very good job of promoting the Trees. Our shows were always in great venues, they were usually sold out, and even though I can't remember what the financial figures were, everyone on our management team seemed to think that Cellar Door was one of the best promoters in the country. Everyone that is, except for Mark. He started to dislike one of the regional promoters in particular, who had been traveling with us from show to show.

I really don't know what the issue was, but it seemed to start the night Mark's black leather coat and some of his personal items were stolen from our backstage dressing room. The local promoter had let a bunch of random people back there when the band wasn't around. Tensions had been building since then, and Mark's drinking was turning into full-blown alcoholism, where he could not remember some of the things he had done the night before. It was an inside joke between all of us when we said: "His mind has shut off, but the body just keeps going!" At which point Mark would imitate himself in a drunken stagger-walk that he had perfected, and we would all laugh hysterically as the sober Mark imitated himself as the drunk Mark.

I have to admit that at this point, my own drinking was also becoming a serious problem. Lee, on the other hand, was as sober as a judge and never drank at all. Lee had only done acid once, in 1986, and apparently that single dose of acid had given Lee everything he ever needed for a lifetime of psychedelic-tinged musical inspiration. And for the record, Lee acted far more professionally than any of the rest of us did, including our crew, and that needs to be stated for the historical record. Lee didn't drink, he didn't do drugs, and he was always ready to play shows to the best of his musical and physical abilities. He played so hard that he blew his knees out and had to start wearing knee braces on stage, but even that didn't slow him down.

Back to the matter of the Florida incident, Mark's fuse finally blew one night when he got into a heated argument with the Cellar Door promoter, and he grabbed the guy by the collar and man-slapped him across the face.

Now to be fair, a slap isn't nearly as damaging as a punch, but its still an assault, and in a way, it's quite a bit more insulting that a punch. That slap tainted our relationship with Cellar Door, even though we were still under contract to play a couple more shows on this leg of the tour. That's when we started to hear a rumor that Cellar Door was going to send a "Golden Gloves boxer" to extract revenge on Mark. We all thought it was a more of a scare tactic than a real threat because if you really were a Golden Gloves boxer, the last thing you'd want to do is sully your reputation with a bare knuckle revenge punch on a lowly rock musician, which might also injure your hands in the process. You wouldn't come across as a professional boxer if you did something like that, but then again, we were on the east coast where we had been attacked once before, and failed boxing contenders often go to work as muscle for the mafia—and the mafia vacations in Florida. Maybe the rumor was true? We all thought we'd better be ready.

Well, the revenge attack did indeed happen, and it happened right after the Trees played our last show with Cellar Door in Florida. We were leaving the backstage area to get on our bus, but we had to walk across a huge dance floor where a disco nightclub was in full swing. This is a ridiculous way for a band to have to exit a venue, but it was par for the Trees. I was walking a few feet behind Mark as we waded through the crowd, when out of the sea of people came a guy who sucker punched Mark straight on the nose. Mark went down on the dance floor and before any of us could comprehend what had just happened, the guy ran off through the crowded club and was gone into the night.

The punch had broken Mark's nose, and as I remember, we had to cancel a couple of shows as a result. This is because anyone who has ever had a broken nose will attest that it is extremely painful to speak with the vibrations that go through the nasal cavity, much less singing in front of a loud rock band.

Once again, the instant karma that Mark often joked about had come back to get him, and it was much worse than the initial slap he had given the lazy promoter.

This whole series of events only served to make the myth of the Screaming Trees be more about fighting than songwriting. The press wrote about it, MTV commented on it, and our reputations as hard drinking street fighters began to precede us more than our songwriting abilities, or the magnificent album we had just released. Instead of being regarded as tunesmiths, we were now thought of as goons who happened to get lucky with our current album.

The Trees never worked with Cellar Door Promotions ever again.

AN INCREDIBLY BAD DECISION

During the three years between 1992–1994, the Trees were almost perpetually on tour. We rarely went back to Seattle for anything other than a short break or the Christmas/New Year holidays when the music business effectively shuts down. We usually went from the end of one tour right into the beginning of another, and this was somewhat eased by the fact that we finally had our own tour bus, which was paid for by tour support from our label. Back then, a bus cost about $1,000 a day, a huge sum at the time, and I'm sure its much more today. Plus there was the driver's salary, diesel fuel, and the various costs of operating a bus—it's massive. But when you are constantly on the move, driving from one city to the next, usually during the night, a tour bus is pretty much a mandatory piece of equipment. Thus, we were in the paradox of having to keep touring to pay for the things that kept us touring.

We also flew quite a bit, mostly for press and radio junkets, or to meet with our label in New York City. We made the flight from SeaTac to JFK airport in New York more times than I can count, and that flight often continued on to London, where our press officer, Matt Reynolds, would cheerfully greet us at our hotel. Matt knew that a large amount of drinking would go hand in hand with whatever interviews and press duties he had lined up for the Trees, but we loved Matt and we trusted him, and he kept stride with us at every turn. I think he loved the Trees as much as anyone in the world.

Those first US and European tours for *Sweet Oblivion* generally had us headlining, with local and regional bands opening for us. We would also play shows where we opened for bigger bands, like the show we played at the Roseland Ballroom in New York City opening for Alice

In Chains in 1992. This particular show had many celebrities in the audience, including the singer Lenny Kravitz. Lenny came backstage after the show to say hello and tell us how much he loved the Trees. He then asked if I would go have a drink with him at a nearby bar, which of course I accepted.

At the bar, we talked about what was happening in this new alternative universe that we were creating. Lenny had a new album coming out titled, *Are You Gonna Go My Way* (1993), and I could tell he was interested in me as a drummer, because he was very complimentary about my playing, informing me that he too had started out as a drummer. Something was definitely afoot between us, but I never found out what it was until almost 25 years later when I ran into Lenny again. It was only then, in 2017, when he told me he had called our new manager to offer me the drum spot in his band.

It was right around that time, in early 1993, that Kim White had left as our manager. There was just too much self-created chaos in our band, and Kim had a legitimately big job at Geffen Records that she needed to prioritize and we all understood this. The temporary manager who had been assigned to us was a greasy, sleazy interim manager who we could immediately tell was not to be trusted. Mark and I referred to him as the "Slick Willy," and this snake in the grass never relayed Lenny Kravitz's offer to me. That's when a bad manager can be your worst enemy, because if I had known what was going to happen to the Screaming Trees in the ensuing years, I probably would have jumped at the chance to play with Lenny Kravitz. But in 1992, I didn't have a clue what was going to happen, or maybe I just didn't want to look at the evidence that was being laid out like breadcrumbs along the trail to Hades' underworld.

When *Sweet Oblivion* was released in September of 1992, we had just launched into a full North American tour with the excellent New York band, Luna, which was a kind of supergroup made up of indie rockers from bands like Galaxy 500, The Feelies, and The Chills. Luna was a New York City band through and through, even though two of the band members were actually from New Zealand. We loved their music, it was cool and laid back with great songwriting at its core, and they had superb vocal melodies with beautiful, overlapping guitar parts.

Luna opened for the Trees on that entire US tour because they had also just released their debut album. The power of our two bands playing together, combined with our new music, made all of our shows sell out. Luna's bassist, Justin Harwood, would even join the Trees on stage for encores, doing a rendition of the Velvet Underground's, "What Goes On." Years later, Justin and I would form our own band, Tuatara, but on this tour we just had fun playing rock & roll together.

Our audience members were as diverse as our musical influences, and I distinctly remember one show in particular, where the meet and greet after party had a mixture of college professors and Hells Angels—and they all got along. The Hells Angels were opening beers for the college professors and they were all sharing stories, as they stood in a circle, everyone laughing together. Everyone seemed to love what the Trees were doing, and a person's professional background had nothing to do with it—the Trees were the people's band. And actually when you think about it, Hell's Angels and college professors have more in common than you might think: the bikers live outside the norms of conventional society, and college professors teach people about how the norms of society are influencing them.

On our tour bus, Mark started calling me by the nickname, "High Country" or just "Country," as an abbreviation. This came from an album cover that we saw at a truck stop, where the singer was wearing a Levis jacket and cowboy boots, which was my automatic outfit on any given day. I had been wearing this exact look since high school and college, and I wasn't about to change it now.

I have to say, I have very fond memories of the Trees at that time, when the band was feeling good, we were playing great shows, and Mark had a humorous twinkle in his eye when he'd say, "Country, come back here to the back of the bus, I want to play you something," at which point Mark would play me some obscure yet amazing folk song that I had never heard before. That was when the music fueled us, rather than the booze, or maybe it was just a combination of the two.

It was after those initial tours in 1992 that things started to go sideways. Because building up to that period of time, the Trees were playing the largest clubs and some of the largest theaters in the United States and Europe. We were selling them out and building an enormous buzz around the world with our lightning bolt live performances. We had several more headline shows on the books at some of the largest venues across America, and that's right when we were offered an opening slot with Alice In Chains.

Now, to preface this with truth and clarity, we all loved Alice In Chains, both as a band and personally as our fellow Seattle brethren. Their 1992 album, *Dirt,* is an incredible album, a verifiable grunge masterpiece, and one of my personal favorites. This proposed tour was pitched to us because Alice was on Columbia Records and the Trees were on Epic Records, both of which were under the Sony Music umbrella. The Sony executives in New York thought it would be a good idea for both of our bands to tour together, which also made their jobs easier from a marketing perspective. The problem was that the Trees were already headlining bigger venues than the Alice guys were, so we would be taking a big step backwards to open for them inside the same venues we had previously sold out, or were about to play as headliners on our own upcoming tour.

The entire thing made no sense to me, and I argued against it for the obvious reasons I just explained. At one point, Gary Lee and I were in a limousine with a couple of Sony executives from the New York office, but we didn't know they worked for Sony—we thought they were radio promoters who were just along for the ride. I started talking about how backwards the Alice/Trees tour would be and Lee said something like, "Well those dip shits at Sony don't even listen to the records they promote, and this tour is just because they want their jobs to be easier." The limousine got very quiet for a time, and of course the word got back to Sony that the Trees were not only a trouble making band, but we were also ungrateful.

The next day, we got a call from the "Slick Willy" manager who said that we had insulted the label and now we had to apologize to make things right. Lee and I refused.

If I'm being totally honest, there were about two or three people at Epic Records who we really liked and who seemed to know the music industry pretty well. We tried to work with those people directly and avoided the others because the vast majority of people who worked at major labels back then were really just hanger-ons, who didn't know very much about the music they were promoting, yet they wanted to live the rock & roll lifestyle vicariously through the bands they represented. From our perspective, the rock & roll lifestyle seemed to be endless nights on a tour bus, with a blur of shows that left us exhausted every night.

From my experience, the Sony executives seemed to be about as smart as a box of hammers, but they were also exactly that—hammers who hammered away until they got their way, even if it was a terrible idea. Up to that point, the Trees were on the upswing, and we were headlining bigger and bigger venues—it was the obvious thing for us to do that because the Trees were naturally a headlining type of band. Some bands are just like that, they are obviously supposed to be headliners, whereas other bands are perpetually openers. For the Screaming Trees to open for Alice In Chains at this point in our career seemed like a deliberately foolish U-turn, even if we liked the very band we would be opening for. We loved Alice's music, but it was professional suicide for us to open for them when we were already selling out the same venues.

The pressure from Sony was enormous: the Trees had to do the Alice tour or there would be serious repercussions. We might get dropped from the label, or at the very least, they wouldn't promote our album anymore, despite the raving critical acclaim and our growing sales numbers. We realized we weren't going to win this battle, and if we didn't do the tour with Alice, all of our tour support would be cut, including for the tour we were about to headline on our own. Sony was playing serious hardball, and we expected that there was other maneuvering going on behind the scenes that we were never told about. Ultimately, the order went out to cancel all of the Trees headlining shows, in all of those big beautiful theaters where we would have thrived. Instead, we got ready to open for Alice In Chains in nightclubs that we had already played.

This was, for me, the moment when the dream of being a totally original band of songwriters, that could hold an audience's attention for three hours, was ultimately steamrolled by the corporate suits at Sony. They could only imagine one big, dumb, package tour that made their jobs as easy as possible.

I would like to be able to say that the tour ended up being an awesome tour where everything went like clockwork, but it wasn't, and it didn't. And again, I have to separate the differences between loving the guys in Alice In Chains, and the awfulness of their tour production. The Alice guys were our friends from Seattle and they probably loved having the Trees as their opener. But what was originally proposed as a band-friendly tour of fellow Seattleites, suddenly became the Trees being treated like second-class citizens when the Alice production team took over, which seemed to come straight out of the Sunset Strip, circa 1983.

In particular was their production manager, who was a full-grown adult man-baby, with a blonde, bowl haircut, coke bottle glasses, and ridiculous red overalls that he seemed to wear every day on the 9 month tour. He really looked more like a circus clown than a production manager, except that he was loud and moody, and he would scream and throw tantrums if someone ate the last stale donut at the coffee station, as I once did. He also had those completely lame "butt rock" tactics up his sleeve, like giving the Trees a broom closet for a dressing room, or setting up the stage so that the curtains in front of the Alice back line fell directly on my drums. In particular, and at our homecoming show in Seattle, the stage curtains fell almost directly on my shoulders so that I would have a difficult time playing in front of our hometown audience.

This was the kind of dunce that had been hired to produce our shows, and this was the kind of petty dipshittery that the Trees had to deal with on a daily basis. On top of this, we were paid nearly nothing as the opening band, so we all had to take a pay cut instead of the raise that we would have gotten if we had done our own headlining tour.

The tour had started in the late fall of 1992 and went well into 1993, as we played dozens of shows across the US, Canada, and eventually Europe. Every show was of course sold out and the press loved it, sometimes writing that the Trees stole the show with our explosive live performance, which we often did. But the effect it had on us as an opening band weakened our position as a headliner, as we were now reduced to playing a simple 40-minute opening set. That kind of tour makes a band become weak, and I can honestly say that I generally disliked every show that I had to play on that tour, but I bit my tongue and did the best I could, waiting for the day when the Trees would headline our own shows again.

One of the biggest shows we played on that tour was that show in New York City at the Roseland Ballroom, when Lenny Kravitz came to meet us. It was probably the single most important show of the entire tour because Sony Music's CEO, Tommy Mottola, and all of his label presidents were attending. The whole point of that show was to demonstrate to Sony what a great live band the Screaming Trees really were. Unfortunately, we failed mightily in our attempt, largely because Mark had been on a massive drinking binge the night before the show, drinking up all of the gin and tonics that could be poured at the Bowery hipster bar, *Max Fish*. It was close to sunrise when we left the bar, and we almost got jumped by a couple tough guys as we stood on the sidewalk waiting for a taxi. I hailed a taxi for Mark, which he got into with a couple women, and I assumed he was heading back to his hotel room, but he didn't—he went to some after party that was just getting started at sunrise.

Later that night at the Roseland Ballroom, Mark was so hung over that he was throwing up in a garbage can on the side of the stage, in between our songs. It was a terrible show for us, and with that, I don't think anyone at Sony took us very seriously anymore, even though we had agreed to do that damn Alice In Chains tour.

1993 was the beginning of a downward spiral that the Screaming Trees would never recover from. We had buckled to the predictively dumb ideas at Sony, and we sold ourselves short as an easily forgotten opening act, right at the moment when we should have been capitalizing on the momentum for *Sweet Oblivion*.

There was also an insane amount of drug abuse on that Alice tour, and I did cocaine for the first and only time in Germany, which had been given to me by our newly appointed, highly incompetent Scottish tour manager. He told me that it would help me get my energy back, it didn't, and fortunately I realized in that one horrible experience what a totally stupid and ridiculous drug cocaine is. Also, that having an incompetent tour manager was worse than having no tour manager at all.

Then there is the well-known fact that Mark and Layne Staley, the singer for Alice In Chains, started using heroin together, something that I also witnessed firsthand. On more than a few occasions, they asked me to accompany them as a kind of bodyguard when they needed to get heroin from the various dope houses across Europe. There I saw zombie-like heroin addicts, passed out in the hallways of "shooting galleries," the needles still stuck in their arms. This was a dire warning of things to come.

This is where, if I can put a positive spin on this, the whole thing becomes like a Zen paradox. This is when a bad thing becomes a blessing that you can't see until much later, after the ordeal has passed. Because doing that Alice tour was a terrible decision for the Screaming Trees professionally, in fact, we never fully recovered from it. Our reputation as headliners had been ruined, and Mark and Layne's individual heroin problems only got worse.

On the other hand, I had become friends with Layne on that tour in a different way than just being the drummer in the opening band. That friendship culminated with our collaboration in Mad Season about a year and half later. I also knew that I never wanted to do hard drugs after what I had seen, even though I had walked through darkened European cities with Layne and Mark when they were not in their best mental or physical condition. But in some strange way, those dark walks had bonded us together in a different kind of way.

And darkness became the overriding mood in the Screaming Trees.

ACT II

DESCENSION

ALTERNATIVE DE-TOURS

By the time the Alice/Trees tour finally concluded in the spring of 1993, everyone was completely and thoroughly burned out, including the band and all the guys in our crew. There were a few highlights however, as there always are even in dark times, like the invitation we got to play *The Tonight Show with Jay Leno*. This time the show's musical director actually wanted me to play drums, so I was finally able to make my TV show debut as a drummer rather than as a food taster, as I had been on David Letterman's show the previous year.

The song we played for *The Tonight Show* was "Dollar Bill," which at the time was climbing up the radio charts. I don't think our performance was particularly great, but it was passable—TV shows aren't really conducive to great live performances. However, in the backstage greenroom, I did get to meet one of my childhood heroes, the actor James Garner. He was a TV and film actor who had starred in countless westerns, WWII movies, and of course the legendary TV series, *The Rockford Files*. Mr. Garner was a total gentleman, and he had in his dressing room a single bottle of Jack Daniels whiskey, with one glass placed at the center of a round black table, and nothing else. It was like a shrine to the gentleman/tough guy archetype that only served to reinforce my belief that alcohol was my appropriate drug of choice. When we were introduced backstage, Mr. Garner said, "Nice to meet you son. What kind of music are you boys gonna play tonight?" To which I replied, respectfully, "The best kind, sir."

It wasn't long before the Trees were on the road again, this time doing another god-forsaken opening spot for what was definitely the worst musical lineup I have ever played in my life—the MTV Alternative Nation Tour.

This was another one of those tours that came out of the boneheaded Sony think tank because all three bands on the tour were signed to one of the various Sony labels. The tour was to be headlined by the absolutely ridiculous, Spin Doctors, who had a couple of hippy jam band songs that had weirdly become radio hits.

The only thing that made this tour remotely tolerable was the Minneapolis band, Soul Asylum, who were playing the middle slot. Soul Asylum had started on the indie label, Twin Tone, which had more in common with Sub Pop than Sony. Minneapolis was kind of a sister city to Seattle, and Soul Asylum were, at their core, great songwriters.

The 30-odd shows we did on that tour were held in giant outdoor amphitheaters known as *sheds,* which exist on the outskirts of almost every major city. These sheds can hold upwards of 30,000 people or more, but that doesn't really help the opening band because when the Trees went out to play our set, only a few hundred people were present at any given show. The audiences we were playing to weren't even close to the numbers we had played to opening for Alice In Chains, not to mention the audiences we had when we were headliners. We were now playing at 5 or 6 pm in the early evening for a few hundred people who came to see the Spin Doctors, but tolerated the Trees as mild entertainment. Our opening set was now only 30 minutes, so by the time we were actually warmed up it was time to leave the stage. Needless to say, we tried to be loaded up and rolling out of town long before the Spin Doctors took the stage.

Another anomaly on this tour was the presence of the actress Winona Ryder, who at the time was dating Dave Pirner, the lead singer of Soul Asylum. Miss Ryder was frequently backstage at the shows, and she was every bit as cool and elegant as you would expect her to be, which is why we were all flabbergasted when she asked to ride on our tour bus from time to time. Of course we obliged, and we behaved much more gentlemanly in her presence—classy ladies have a tendency to bring about this kind of character improvement with bruisers like us.

This was around the same time that celebrities were starting to show up at our shows, and we once read in a magazine that Uma Thurman had said that the Screaming Trees were one of her favorite bands. Everything seemed to be cool on the outside, but on the inside, the

Trees were dying. Those back-to-back opening spots for Alice In Chains and the Spin Doctors were absolutely soul-crushing exercises in musical futility. More importantly, we saw from our slumping sales figures that it was, in fact, a terrible idea for the Trees to be an opening act for anyone. When the Trees headlined, we sold albums and the buzz grew, but when we opened for other bands, we didn't sell any records and people seemed disinterested in us. We were treading water, literally, wasting tour support money on tours that weren't helping us at all, and the band was losing moral by the day.

It's worth mentioning that before we did the criminally misnamed *Alternative Nation Tour*, the Trees had set out to do some headline shows, hoping to get some momentum back. It was different now, because were working from behind the eight ball, rather than being in control of the table as we were in the fall of 1992 when *Sweet Oblivion* had just come out. We were back to playing the clubs again because the previous 18 months of touring had only served to set us back, and had not moved us any closer to the goal line.

For that small run of headline shows, we chose the excellent indie rock band, The Poster Children, as our opener, and we set out on a short run across the US and Canada. To be honest, I can't remember much about those shows, whether they were remarkable or not. The fact that I can't remember anything, even after looking at the tour books with dates and venues, tells me that it was an unremarkable tour. What I do remember, however, was an absolutely awful experience in Montreal, Quebec on May 3rd, 1993.

It was after that show when a bartender at the venue, *The Backstreet Club*, broke a beer bottle across the face of Poster Children drummer, John Herndon. We loved John, he was a fantastic drummer and a wonderful guy to hang out with. His nickname on the tour was "Spider" and he was kind of short in stature, but he had a huge heart and superb drumming skills. For anyone to attack him was absolutely unconscionable to the Trees, and when I saw him stumbling out of the venue, all cut up with blood running down his face, I thought to myself, this is not right by any of the laws of the Universe—revenge must be taken.

I was enraged and half-screaming as John gave me a description of the guy behind the bar, and it sounded like he had just gotten off work and decided to pick a fight on his way out the door.

I found the guy almost immediately and had him cornered, his shirt clenched in my fist as I screamed, "Did you do it, did you break the bottle on John's face?" The guy was terrified, but he didn't deny it either, it was definitely him, and I was about to pummel him when an arm snaked around from behind, tightening around my neck. It was a sleeper hold that one of the bouncers had put on me, trying to protect his fellow degenerate. "Get out of here!" I heard the bouncer say to his friend, as the coward ran for the door. I was struggling to get out of the hold, stomping on the bouncer's instep but it wasn't working very well, and then suddenly, the mighty Van Conner appeared, who, when he wanted to be, was as powerful as a rhinoceros. Van, with one hand, twisted the bouncer's arm off my neck, as I regained my footing to counterattack, but by this time the bottle-smasher had fled.

I was so infuriated that this club would allow their own employees to assault musicians who had just played there, and then help them escape. I swore vengeance, but to this day I have not been able to fulfill it. There was nothing alternative or culturally enriching about this kind of touring. We were just playing dingy, low level clubs in cities across the US and Canada, and anyone can do that.

We were becoming the steakhouse band, that Mark had warned us about.

WARPAINT

I wish I could say that the Trees finally went home, got sober, and then made another brilliant album, except that's not what happened. Instead, our raging alcoholism had become a new kind of normal for us, and as we stayed out on the road, our maniacal behavior become even more so.

By 1994, which was really only the first three years of my decade in the Screaming Trees, my own alcoholism had reached its apex. It's alternately fascinating and revolting on how damaging that disease can be to the mind and body. In my case, as with most alcoholics, it was always there, it was just waiting to be genetically released. The Trees relentless touring schedule was the perfect opportunity for this to happen, because I drank every day of my life, without ever thinking about it. Most of the time, no one even noticed, but I was generally a good natured drunk. However on my worst nights, I made a fool of myself, and in one particular incident, it also involved a bladed weapon, used in the most unskillful of ways.

You see, before every show on that Alice In Chains tour, there was a weapons confiscation system that was set up at the entry points to every venue. This was to prevent someone from bringing in a gun, or a knife, or any kind of lethal weapon. There were boxes and boxes of these things, the vast majority of which were knives, and I'm not sure if any guns were confiscated, but I wouldn't be surprised if there had been. At some point, these boxes of weapons were given to our tour managers for the band and crew to pick out whatever souvenir they wanted to keep. I wasn't there when the weapon-picking happened, but Layne had chosen one for me—a beautiful butterfly knife with mother of pearl handles that had a long straight razor for its blade. As Layne handed it to me he said something like, "Here ya go Bear, this seems like your kind of style." Maybe he heard me talking about Kung Fu, even though I had zero training in knife fighting techniques.

I started playing with the knife, learning a few of the ways to spin it open and closed, something I had actually seen years earlier from a friend in high school who had one of these contraptions. I was getting to be pretty good at it, but that was only when I was sober.

Late one night, after another unmemorable show, in some unmemorable city, our bus driver decided to stop at a truck stop for dinner or breakfast, depending on the meal you desire at 3 am. I had been drinking all day and all night for a couple days and was absolutely the most mentally deranged that I had ever been in my life. I never wanted any of the bullshit hard drugs that were rampantly available at any show, I just wanted booze, whiskey in particular, and usually with a beer chaser. I had already consumed a vast amount of this particular combination, so by the time we arrived at the truck stop, I was completely blind drunk.

I staggered off the bus and sat down at a table with some of the crew guys, and I was able to order some food assisted by our tour manager, Danny Baird, who was sitting next to me. I then excused myself to use the bathroom because I desperately needed to pee. The butterfly knife was in the front pocket of my jeans, unforgotten until I felt it with my hand, as I swayed in front of the urinal. I pulled it out and for reasons that I can only attribute to so many consecutive years on the road, in vans and busses, crammed with people I sometimes didn't like, with little or no sleep and way to much alcohol, I came up with the brilliant idea of slicing horizontal cuts on my face, so as to create streaks of blood, or, *warpaint* as I like to think of it.

I know it's an insane idea, but it seemed reasonable at the time, and I thought the crew guys might get a laugh out of it.

I came out of the bathroom with my bloodied warpaint face, and as I re-entered the restaurant full of truck and bus drivers I screamed out, "I'll take on all of you motherfuckers!" I actually remember this quite clearly because of the way everyone in the restaurant turned around and looked at me in disbelief. There was a brief moment of pause, and then everyone went right back to eating their meals as if they had seen my kind of idiocy plenty of times before.

Any one of them could have easily knocked me out with a single punch to the chin, but they didn't, and fortunately I had the good sense to put the knife back in my pocket before I made my bold proclamation, else someone might have shot me as well.

I was incapable of doing anything except making a complete ass of myself, as I stumbled back to my table to sit down and eat my unappetizing breakfast. In my drunken state, I distinctly remember hearing one of the drivers say, "I like that boy a lot, but he has totally lost his mind this time."

Our tour manager, Danny Baird, said with no small amount of disgust in his voice, "Give me that goddamn knife!" to which I meekly handed it over to him. He relayed it to me years later that he simply tossed the knife in the garbage can on our way back to the bus.

I passed out in my bunk, and when I sobered up the next day, Mark Lanegan took me aside and said in a surprisingly gently way, "Jesus man, you really went all the way last night. When you came out of the bathroom with all that blood on your face, you looked like the wild boar on the Gordon's gin bottle. I think you might have a little drinking problem brother," he said with a quizzical grin.

Let me repeat that: Mark Lanegan told me that I might have a drinking problem.

And that's when I knew it was time to sober up.

INJURIES OF THE TRADE

Aside from slashing their faces with a straight razor, any band that has been on tour for any amount of time can attest to the large number of ills one can suffer from on the road. It's simply the nature of the beast to be out there in the greater world, playing countless shows, shaking hands with strangers, and eating food that is prepared and consumed under usually less than ideal conditions. Such was the case with the Screaming Trees, including the various injuries we sustained on the road.

These numerous health issues seemed to come in waves, the most common of which is a digestive plague that we came to call, "Crippleton's Diarrhea." We gave it the name Crippleton's because it sounded like a Victorian-era diagnosis that came from the crippling effects of diarrhea. This usually came from eating a bad meal somewhere on the road, and it often came as a cluster infection if the band and crew ate together at the same dingy place, and then all of us would experience a group case of the Crippleton's. Even I, who had a famously iron stomach and could eat almost anything without ill effect, had several cases of Crippleton's during my tenure in the Trees. It was just an accepted fact that sooner or later, a bout of the Crippleton's would eventually strike.

With physical, bodily injuries, the band seemed to run a dead heat with all of us suffering from numerous leg and ankle injuries. Lee was constantly blowing out his knees on stage because of his explosive live performances, which required that he use knee braces and a cane from time to time.

Mark was in and out of emergency rooms with various infections in his arms, as well as an ankle injury he sustained when he jumped of the stage in pursuit of a shithead who had thrown a coin that hit Mark in the face. Mark tackled him in the crowd and meted out the appropriate punishment, however, the jump off the stage cracked his ankle, which required that he use a stool on stage for a time, and then a cane for months afterwards.

Van also hurt his leg or ankle (which one I can't remember) and he too was using a cane for a time. I had already broken my left ankle on the last night of the 1992 European tour, which also required that I use a cane off and on. The irony is that the Tree were all in our mid to late 20s, yet here we were, constantly getting injured like old men, and all of us were using canes!

Van gave us a particularly bad scare once when he started having severe chest pains, which sent him to the emergency room and we were all very worried that he might be having a heart attack. Fortunately, the attending cardiologist determined that it was just stress related tension—and this seemed obvious considering the conditions we were touring under.

Then there was the infamous time on the Alice/Trees tour when we were in Canada, and Mark's arm had become severely infected from bad heroin he had bought in Montreal, which developed into blood poisoning. Mark's arm was swelling up to a frightening degree, so that by the time we got him to the emergency room, his arm was twice the size as his other arm.

The Canadian doctors were none to pleased with an American rock star doing heroin in their country, and Mark told us that the emergency room doctor told him that the Canadian drug dealers often cut their heroin with dog shit, to cause this exact effect on foreign drug addicts in their country. After seeing Mark's massively infected arm in the emergency room, this seemed like a probable cause. Then we saw the black marker line that the doctor had drawn on his arm, telling Mark that they might have to amputate it, should the reddening infection grow beyond the black line. We were all terrified of what might happen, and we stayed at a nearby hotel waiting for news. Fortunately for Mark, the infection stopped right at the black line, and a few days later he was released from the hospital.

This is also the reason why there is video footage of Layne Staley singing with the Screaming Trees in Montreal because we were already set up on stage and ready to play our opening set when Mark was rushed to the hospital. We did a few songs as a trio, and then Layne jumped onstage to sing "Nearly Lost You" with us. It was a ragged set to be sure, but we pulled it off while Mark lay on a gurney in the emergency room.

Unfortunately, and because of all the drug decadence that escalated on that tour, Mark was usually sick from the ill effects of heroin use, or the terrible withdrawal symptoms when he couldn't get it. This made him "dope sick" when heroin was not available, and that's when he would turn to methadone, which is a pharmaceutically made heroin substitute that is equally damaging. Needless to say—and Mark has already written the definitive treatise on the subject, but he was pretty sick for the last few years we were on the road.

The last medical emergency that happened to me was when we were playing on that god-forsaken *MTV Alternative Nation Tour,* somewhere on the east coast. This incident also involved my drum tech, John Hicks, who needs a little background story himself.

John was from Tennessee, and he had an extremely sharp and wicked sense of humor like many Southerners have, which made him famous with every band we ever toured with. He had the ability to do impersonations of almost every prominent TV and film character, with the equally impressive ability to recite their lines, verbatim.

For example, once when he was in the elevator of our hotel in Chattanooga, TN, John randomly met the actor, Don Knotts—he even got his picture taken with him. This led to John doing endless impersonations of Don Knotts in his Barney Fife character, which John modified to fit unlimited scenarios, and this went on for literally years.

Because of John's ability to entertain the band and crew as we rolled down the endless highways of the world, he became more valuable as our comedic relief, and his work as my drum tech became a secondary responsibility. If I could have given John career advice back then, I would have insisted that he become a stand up comedian rather than a roadie because he was that talented.

And so it happened, one morning after John had a particularly wild night, I found him polishing my cymbals, scrubbing away on a road case by the side of the stage. "Look how much dirt came off!" he exclaimed, as I walked up to greet him. It was only then that I realized he had been polishing my cymbals—all of them, with a set of metal Brillo pads. These were the kind you use to clean extremely dirty cast iron skillets, and John had completely scratched up and destroyed an entire set of cymbals, about $2,000 worth.

They sounded as dead as garbage can lids when I hit them, because the tonal grooves had been destroyed by John's furious scrubbing. Since this was my only set of cymbals, I had to play them for a couple of shows until Sabian Cymbals could ship me out a new set. I was infuriated with John, so for the next few days I told him to steer clear of my drums while I did the tech work myself, and I suggested he work on some comedy sketches to redeem himself.

While John worked on his comedy routine, I replaced all the drum heads on my kit, which had come in a very dirty cardboard box that looked as if it had been shipped across the country in a horse drawn wagon. In the course of opening the box, I cut my left thumb on the dirty cardboard. No big deal I thought, it didn't even really bleed since it was more like a paper cut. It was a few days later when I felt like my thumb was about to explode and self-amputate itself from my hand.

I had been sleeping in my bunk on the bus, waking up from time to time because of the intense throbbing in my thumb. When I finally awoke in the late morning the next day, we had already arrived at the venue and I could see that my thumb was enormously swollen, three times its normal size. It looked like a giant, rubber cartoon thumb that a clown might use, and it was crimson red from the terrible infection.

I'd never had this happen before because I had been cut and gashed so many times during my childhood growing up on a small farm in the woods of Washington State—I never got infections. I figured my body could fend off almost anything, but apparently not in this case because my thumb was hurting so badly that it was impossible for me to hold anything in my left hand, much less a drumstick. Sound check was only a couple hours away, and that's when our tour manager, Danny Baird, called for one of the on-site paramedics to come backstage and assess the situation.

"Yeah, his thumb is badly infected, it looks like it has a big abscess inside of it," the medic said. "I can lance it, but it's gonna hurt like hell." He then showed me his lancing tool, which was a small metal trough with a razor sharp point that made a path for the blood and pus to drain out.

"Let's do it," I said, "I can't take it anymore, it feels like I'm in a thumbscrew and I can't play a show like this."

The medic took me outside to where the light was better in the hot sun. He then positioned himself in front of me, with his back to my chest, so it was more like I was hugging him from behind. He then took his left arm and wrapped it around my left arm like some kind of Jiu Jitsu arm lock. He started squeezing my thumb from the palm upward, which was excruciating. That's when he said, "Get ready, I'm going to count to three."

He was squeezing my thumb so tightly I thought it might rupture from the pressure, as he counted down, "One, two…" and before he got to three I felt the stab.

God damn it hurt, because you've got more nerves in your fingertips and toes than almost the rest of your body combined—that's why fingers and toes were the main point of torture amongst the Catholic inquisitors. In the same instant that the lance sliced deep into my thumb, I heard a loud popping noise as the thumb ejected the accumulated pus from the infection. I heard the medic say, "Oh boy…."

The medic continued to drain my thumb, working out a steady flow of goo onto the concrete. The pain was much less now, and when he finally stopped to put an antibiotic on the wound and wrap it in a bandage, I was so relieved that I started laughing. It was only then that I saw the amount of blood and pus that had shot six feet across the concrete walkway. "It looks like a crime scene," I said, "but thank you so very much." The medic laughed as he finished patching me up, "That's what we're here for," and then he headed back down to his medic station, where I'm sure he treated more people that night who were drunk, on drugs, and who knows what. Thank god for those medics—they keep the shows going forward, and they've certainly seen far worse than my infected thumb.

And so, with a couple of painkillers and a shot of whiskey, I was ready to hold a drumstick again and play our show that night, even though it was another meaningless opening set on a tour that we should have never agreed to do in the first place.

Thus we soldiered onward, playing as best as we could, despite the ongoing injuries of our trade.

MUSICAL ABORTIONS

It was now well into 1994, and the Screaming Trees were finally nearing the end of our touring cycle for *Sweet Oblivion*, which had lasted for two and half years. If I counted the two years I had been on tour with Skin Yard right before I joined the Trees, I had been on the road for almost 5 continuous years. I was thoroughly burned out, and so were the other guys. Still, we had to start thinking about making another album to follow up *Sweet Oblivion* because in rock & roll, you have to keep the momentum going when you are trying to break through into the mainstream. We were so close, but we hadn't quite cracked the ceiling yet.

I suppose the brighter side of the equation was that *Sweet Oblivion* had sold about 350,000 LPs and CDs, and although we didn't have a gold or platinum album yet, it was by far the highest selling album that the Trees had ever made, outselling its predecessors by a factor of ten to one. When we did the math on it, we figured that Sony had made at least $10.00 per unit on each of those sales, making them a tidy profit of 3 or 4 million dollars just from that one album alone. They weren't losing money on the Trees at all, but they weren't making the massive profits they had hoped for either. But as every label executive will tell you, the bread and butter comes from a whole bunch of little bands, making a little bit of money all the time, which keeps the record label flush with cash.

The Trees were approved to make another album, it wasn't even an issue this time, but we still had a lot of ground to make up. It was much like the way we had started with *Sweet Oblivion*—as the underdogs making a comeback album. Or as the great Yankees catcher Yogi Berra once said, "It was déjà vu all over again."

My housemate, Van Conner, had married his girlfriend Jill, and they were now living together in a separate house. I was happy for them, we all were, because they were perfect for each other. Before I could announce my search for a new roommate, Van informed me that his brother Lee would be taking his place, largely because Lee had to write songs for the next Trees album, and our house was a perfect place for writing. "OK Lee, welcome to the neighborhood."

Gary Lee Conner, born August 22nd, 1962, was a classic Leo. Being that I was an Aries, also a fire sign, we understood each other in that intuitive way that only fire signs do. Our mission on Earth is to create art and let no one stand in our way of doing that. We knew that creativity came in explosive bursts of light and when this happens, you must work diligently to capture it. Lee was constantly writing songs, whether we had an album to record or not, but now he was working at double the pace. I was writing too, buying my first Tascam 4-track cassette recorder, as we worked on new songs in our respective bedrooms. Our goal was to write songs that were better than what we had written for *Sweet Oblivion*, a very tall order, but we could do it. Songwriting is supposed to be an ever-improving exercise.

I think it needs to be acknowledged that Lee got a lot of bad commentary in Mark's memoir, and maybe some of it from the early days of the Trees was merited. But all creative relationships are different, as was mine with Lee and Van, and as was mine with Mark. What I saw in Lee was an unswerving dedication to write songs, all the time, in lengthy recording sessions that went for several hours, often late into the night.

Lee would write every day without fail, and he would produce compilation tapes that had upwards of 10-12 songs per tape. No one could say that Lee did not put in a Herculean effort to write the next Trees album. So did Van for that matter, and even I, the drummer, was cranking out the tunes faster than I ever had. Up to that point, I had never really focused on songwriting per se, because when I went to music school as a jazz drummer in the mid 1980s, it was more about arranging and compositional theory. That's a very different approach than sitting down with a guitar and coming up with a chord progression, a melody for the voice, and then writing lyrics. This was new territory for me, but I was hooked on the idea of writing original rock songs and I threw myself into the practice completely.

Since Lee had been the main songwriter of the Trees from their inception, the general conversation was usually about his songs. They often sounded similar, yet one out of every 10 songs Lee would write would be a pretty great song, and every now and then there would be a song that we all thought could be a hit, or at least the potential for one. Van was less prolific than his brother, but even then, Van would deliver a great song out of nowhere like, "Nearly Lost You," which was the Trees first major hit. I even wrote some songs, which Mark said he liked and might make their way onto the next album. It felt like a time of optimism.

I learned so much about songwriting from watching and listening to both Lee and Mark, because they each had unique talents that served to make every song better. When they moved past the petty bickering, which was usually over a minor change in a song, the result was usually a very good song. Mark even attested that it was Lee who taught him how to write songs in the early years of the band, which Mark then took to even greater heights with his own songwriting skill.

Aside from that falling refrigerator incident in Cincinnati, Lee and I never had a single conflict between us, whether at home as roommates, or out on the road with the Trees. He also encouraged me to write more songs, giving me different bits of advice on techniques and little tricks that he would employ. Often my song ideas became additional parts in songs that Lee or Mark were already writing, and it was in that little house near Green Lake where we came up with the basic foundation for what was going to be our next album.

Our A&R rep, Bob Pfeifer, approved and expanded our budget to record again with *Sweet Oblivion* producer, Don Fleming, and the same engineer, John Agnello. We decided to stay in Seattle this time, as we all had girlfriends and wives that we had not spent enough time with in our previous years on the road. We picked a studio called *Bad Animals* on 4th avenue in downtown Seattle, a studio which had been around since the 1970s, and had been recently purchased and renovated by the Wilson sisters of the Seattle band, Heart. We set up to record the basic tracks in Studio A, where many great bands had recorded in the past, and we thought (or rather, hoped) that the same magic would arise within us.

For whatever reason, the recording sessions at *Bad Animals* were just not as inspired as the *Sweet Oblivion* sessions in New York City. And although we had some very good songs written between us, if we were truly honest, it was clear that the songs weren't as fully realized as they should have been. They were great songs, we just needed more time to perfect them before recording them.

Maybe it was because we had spent the previous two and half years touring the world instead of writing and rehearsing the songs *before* we got into the studio. As it was, we were essentially working on the songs in demo form, and then learning how to play them as a band in the tracking room. So instead of the tight, concise arrangements that we had created for *Sweet Oblivion* in my old Jackson Street warehouse loft, we were now recording basic tracks with fluid arrangements that could be edited to match whatever lyrics Mark eventually came up with. This was partly because Mark wasn't attending the recording sessions as frequently as he had in New York, and he didn't have his lyrics ready. It was becoming apparent that his heroin addiction, which had been turbocharged on the Alice In Chains tour, was now taking precedent over all other things in his life.

As any true songwriter or recording artist knows, this is not the right way to record a song, or an album for that matter. A band shouldn't be cutting basic tracks until they have tight arrangements and some amount of lyrics that are pretty close to being done, at least to the degree that they can operate as placeholders until the final lyrics are sung.

The end result of all this, was that we had an album of pretty great basic tracks, but Mark had only finished vocals for 9 songs, and Van and Lee had sung on 3 more, out of the approximately 15 songs that we had tracked for the album.

After sending what we had completed to Bob Pfeifer and Epic Records, the label's consensus was that we should wrap up the sessions and try again at a later date when the band was more rested. Most of that decision came from the Trees themselves, because we knew that we were burned out and needed to take a break to write and rehearse more songs. That's because when you take songwriting as seriously as we did, you also have to have the self-awareness to know when you have real gold on your hands, or when you are cranking out lead.

A wise songwriter knows that it is better to not release something sub par, and to wait until you have gold again. And as hard as it was for the Trees to suspend that album and wait for a better creative time to emerge, it was absolutely the right thing to do.

It was also a testament to Epic Records that they kept us on the roster, and were willing to spend a lot of money to let us try again. Maybe they weren't so bad after all, because after our disastrous opening slot tours and the bad-mouthing we had given Sony, the label still knew that the Trees were some of the best songwriters in rock & roll. They were willing to wait for us to produce a great album again, when the time was right.

The recording sessions at *Bad Animals* would later become known as *The Aborted Album*, not because it was a bad album, but because it was an incomplete album. Some of the best songs from that session would end up on a Trees compilation album that Sony released many years later, long after the band had ended.

We would get another chance to make another album the following year, but before any of that could happen, Mark and I would have a very unique and magical adventure with a very different kind of band.

Our season of madness would finally come to its fruition.

'TWAS A MAD SEASON

I want to say at the beginning of this story that I have written extensively about Mad Season in my previous books, as well as the liner notes for the deluxe edition of our seminal album, *Above (1995)*. As a result, this story is another version of that story, which I think is necessary for this book, perhaps with some new insights. For me, Mad Season marked the apex of my recording work in the first half of the 1990s, which included my work with Mark Lanegan, as well as our good friend, Layne Staley. In many ways, Mad Season was a great victory for us all, in that it was the musical reawakening we all needed. It was a kind of side road that we all took together, which resulted in some very different and extremely beautiful music that I don't think any of us could have imagined in the context of our other bands. For that reason alone, it is a moment of ascension in between periods of great darkness. I suppose that's why we named our album *Above,* and I think this is why the album stands out as a classic almost 30 years later.

That album seems to be, from my perspective, the most realized and authentically original album that any of us had made up to that point in our careers. It was, and still is, the best selling album that I have ever participated in as a band member, and I think this is largely because the timeless themes in our songs resonated with so many people back then, as they still do to this day.

The band came together because of a variety of factors, but it really began with a nuclear moment when Mike McCready of Pearl Jam picked up the phone and called me at my home. Mike had been watching the Screaming Trees play shows for a couple of years by that point, and this convinced him of my drumming ability. On top of that, the Screaming Trees had done our 1992-93 world tour with Alice In Chains, which created a musical link between Layne, Mark, and myself. The pieces were slowly coming together, but it was Mike who had the foresight to see our potential when he made that first call to me.

It was now mid 1994, and Seattle and the rest of the world was reeling from the suicide of Kurt Cobain, which had happened on April 5th of that year. A lot of us in the Seattle music scene were questioning what exactly it was that we were doing if the end result could bring about such a horrible outcome for one of our musical heroes.

Mike had recently gotten sober at a rehab facility in Minnesota, where he had bonded with a blues bassist from Chicago named John Baker Saunders. The two of them had recently moved back to Seattle, and that's when Mike asked if I would meet him for dinner at a restaurant in Seattle's Fremont neighborhood. He said wanted to talk about a musical idea that he was considering, but I had no idea what it could be.

We had a great talk about all the touring and traveling we had done in our respective bands, and that's when Mike proposed that we do a side project together that would include this blues bassist he had met in rehab. I loved the idea immediately because I always wanted to play with a guitarist of Mike's caliber, and I also loved the blues. That's when Mike said he also wanted to see if Layne Staley might want to be the singer. Even though I still had some sore spots around that Alice/Trees tour from the previous year, I knew Layne was a once in a generation singer and I really wanted to work with him, but in a totally different scenario.

I had just gotten sober as well, not in a rehab facility, but on my own accord. All of that drinking, smoking, and the general unhealthiness of the road had given me my first bout of post-alcohol depression, which came with an extra care package of anxiety and insomnia. That was the initial trade off I got from not drinking—I couldn't sleep, and my mind was racing all the time. Fortunately, I was living by myself in an upscale apartment that I could finally afford, and the only thing that made me feel remotely sane was walking for miles around Green Lake, my old neighborhood where I used to live and write songs with Van and Lee. Thus, doing a project like Mike had proposed seemed like a gift from the gods, something that could harness my musical ambitions and keep me sane and sober at the same time.

Our initial jams started shortly after that first dinner meeting, with Mike, Baker, and myself convening at Naf Productions, a band rehearsal complex near the Port Of Seattle where many Seattle bands practiced. The three of us jammed as a trio for the first couple of times, and we immediately gelled with our musical chemistry. We created some great instrumental jams that were hooky and catchy even without Layne's vocals, which we tried to imagine in his absence. After the first two or three trio jams, Layne started coming down as well, and over the course of the following two weeks we refined the songs as Layne started singing the lyrics as they came to him, writing them down in a notebook that he always kept nearby.

I never asked Layne directly if he was clean or not, that would have seemed rude and out of place with the good energy that was developing between us. But at that time, he looked great and seemed relatively healthy, and he was clearly excited to be playing in a new band where he was the only singer, and his lyrical ideas were welcomed into our fold.

We decided that playing a couple unannounced shows might be a good way to try out our new songs, live in front of an audience where we could gauge their reactions to our songs. I suggested *The Crocodile* as the venue, since I had a personal connection there with Peter Buck of R.E.M. and his then wife, Stephanie, who had started the Crocodile back in 1991. This was the best rock club on the west coast and one of the best clubs in the country, where the hippest bands in the world would play whenever their tours brought them through Seattle.

Mad Season played three unannounced shows at *The Crocodile* between October and November of 1994, where we used a rather awful disguise name called, The Gacy Bunch, which was a combination of a serial killer's name and *The Brady Bunch* TV show. Fortunately, we would change our name to Mad Season soon after, but for these three unannounced shows, The Gacy Bunch served its primary purpose, which was to confuse everyone.

After those first three shows, we knew we were ready to go into the studio to make a record, and that's when I made my second appearance at *Bad Animals Studio*, back in the same Studio A where the Trees had tried to record an album earlier that year.

By the time Mad Season entered the studio in late 1994, a slew of notable bands had either finished albums at *Bad Animals*, or were in the process of recording them there: Soundgarden's *Superunknown*

(1994), Alice In Chains' *Dirt (1992)*, Hole's *Live Trough This (1994)*, and
R.E.M.'s *New Adventures In Hi Fi (1996)* were among the albums that
were recorded at *Bad Animals*. The resonate energy in the studio was
palpable, and we were determined to capture some of it for our own
album.

I remember that we tracked the entire album, including all of the
overdubs, in about two weeks time, doing most of the basic tracks live
with all four of us playing together in the same room. This was done on
a Studer 2-inch, 24-track magnetic tape machine, just as we had used
with the Trees, and which by some is still considered the gold standard
for the highest possible recording quality.

After the basic tracks were done, Layne would stay late into the
night to sing his vocals, doing his trademark harmonies in multiple
layers. It was incredible to watch him, and then come back to the studio
the following day and hear what he had done the night before. You see,
Layne had this ability to imagine his vocal performance in its entirety,
with all of the harmonies in their place. He'd then go out into the studio
and sing it perfectly, in real time, layer by layer, with no auto tune
whatsoever. That effect didn't even exist in 1994, so singers back then
had to actually sing. Of all the great singers I have worked with in my
life, and they have all been titans, Layne Staley was truly the most gifted
of them all, both poetically and musically.

The only song that was assembled in layers was a composition I
had written on upright bass that was originally called, "Marimba Song,"
simply because it had a marimba as a key part of the song. We changed
the name to "Long Gone Day," after Layne wrote the chorus, and it
became one of our best-known songs.

I had played upright bass and mallet instruments like vibraphone
and marimba in high school and college, and I wanted to record
something that used these instruments, rather just another song built
around a guitar riff. Plus, I had been frustrated by the Screaming Trees
passing over my own songs during the aborted album sessions, and I
was now playing in a band that happily accepted the music I was writing.
With Mad Season, I saw an opportunity to express a philosophy that
I had been thinking about for quite some time, which is that music
can be heavy without necessarily being loud and distorted. Sometimes
heavy music can be made with acoustic, classical instruments, which
Led Zeppelin taught us in the 1970s.

I didn't know if my experiment would work, but I started the process by arriving at the studio earlier than the other guys so I could try out my idea. I began by laying down the upright bass to a click track that co-producer and engineer, Brett Eliason, had set up for me to play with. Then I added the marimba, some very simple drums, and some congas. Mike later recorded an acoustic guitar, and Brett suggested a local saxophone player named Skerik, who came down to record the tenor sax solos in the two bridge sections. When Layne came into the control room to hear what I had created that day, he immediately loved it and that's when he said, "Why don't we get Mark Lanegan to come down and sing on this too?"

I thought it was a fantastic idea, so Layne called Mark to come down the next night. This turned out to be one of the best things that ever happened with music that Mark and I created together because his vocals on the Mad Season album gave us two incredible songs: "Long Gone Day," and another song I wrote for the album, "Above", which ended up being the title track of the album.

As the sessions neared completion, I told Mark that the band had talked and we all agreed that we wanted to give him a share of the royalties, or *points*, as they are called. He greatly appreciated the gesture because the royalties he received from Mad Season were a lifesaver during some very lean times that bailed him out of some tough financial spots. It did the same for me on many occasions, and I say all this now because this is what friends and band mates are supposed to do for one another—you look out for each other's best interests, both mentally and financially.

As we were getting close to our mixing date, I added some non-traditional sounds to a few songs, like the vibraphone on "Wake Up," which is the opening track of the album, born out of a bass riff that Baker had introduced during our first jam session. I also added some industrial percussion to "I Don't Know Anything", a fantastically heavy song that Layne had written and brought to the band. I also added a cello to "River Of Deceit", a beautiful song that Mike had written in rehab, which would go one to become our biggest hit. That cello part would come back to us in a beautiful way decades later, which I'll explain near the end of this story. All of these rather exotic sounds gave our album a very different sonic quality, so Mad Season wasn't just the traditional instrumentation of drums, bass, guitar, and vocals. It had became much more.

Mixing happened in the adjacent *Studio X*, which was the big, state of the art studio in the *Bad Animals* complex. That's when we began to hear how magical our album was going to sound—it just had this *thing* in it, which is impossible to put in words, yet we could all feel it in our souls. We knew we had struck gold long before the album was ever certified gold.

We also knew that we needed to formalize our name as Mad Season and apply for the trademark. The name itself came from a term that Mike had heard when he was in England with Pearl Jam, around the time when the psychedelic mushrooms sprout from the fields and pastures, a time the English call, *The Mad Season.* We loved the name and it fit the band perfectly, especially because the Pacific Northwest had a similar magic mushroom season, something we had all partaken in. Mad Season was now our official band name, so it was just the artwork that needed to be completed so we could assemble the final packaging.

Layne, being the multi-faceted artist that he was, had been making beautiful black and white etchings that looked like wood block prints, of which he had done a series of three. He submitted these etchings to the band, and one of them totally stood out and we loved it immediately. It was definitely the cover of the album because the image fit the themes of our songs perfectly. Baker, who had an exceptional eye for detail with graphic design, assumed the responsibility of overseeing the vinyl and CD packaging, and within a very short time, our beautiful album was realized, complete with Layne's original artwork and Baker's layout and design. This is exactly how a real band should function, with everyone adding their individual talents to the final creation.

The album was released on March 14th, 1995, exactly one month before my 28th birthday, and it was, considering those pre-Internet times, a fairly instant success, being declared a gold album (500,000 copies sold) in just a few weeks. Now the album is nearly platinum in the United States, with about two million units sold worldwide. People absolutely loved it, and Mike's brilliant song, "River Of Deceit," became a huge hit, reaching #2 on the rock radio chart.

At this point, Mad Season needed to decide if we wanted to play these songs live in a formal concert setting, or maybe we would just keep it as a mysterious studio band, which was something we talked about. We ultimately decided to play live, but there would only be two officially announced shows, both in Seattle. Part of the reason for this was that there really wasn't enough time to do a proper tour with everyone's schedules getting booked up with our regular bands. The other reason is that truly magical things are ephemeral, and they don't last very long.

We announced our first show to be at the Moore Theatre in downtown Seattle, just a few blocks from where we had recorded the album at *Bad Animals*. It sold out within a few minutes. Mike then suggested we film the concert, which was an expensive gamble because of the cost of real, celluloid film—digital cameras didn't exist yet. I remember the film budget being in excess of $100,000, but our label, Columbia Records, gave us the green light to film the show. It turned out to be one of the greatest shows I have ever played in my life, and fortunately it was all captured on film, *Mad Season, Live At The Moore Theatre*.

The second show was in an even smaller venue, held on New Years Eve in 1995 at a club called RKCNDY. That show was filmed and recorded as well, albeit on a smaller 16-millimeter camera. This was fortuitous, especially when we decided to release a deluxe edition box set in 2013, which included these two films, as well as some other recorded rarities. Much of that film footage I had never even seen before, and I was astonished at the band's power on stage.

With almost 30 years behind us, I think I can truly say that Mad Season was a band of exceptional musical ideas that came about because of our decision to get sober, which in turn gave us the courage to try something different. This allowed us to make an album that was absolutely unique from any of the other bands we were playing with at the time, and it gave us a path to a pure artistic vision, without the pressure of a record label or any other outside force. It was just the four of us (five, counting Mark) doing what we wanted to do, and it was absolutely, unequivocally, magical.

The *Above* album did so well that plans were made to record a second album the following year, in 1996. As we had done before, Mike, Baker and I started to record some basic ideas with Brett Eliason at the helm, as we sketched out about 18 basic song ideas. Peter Buck of R.E.M. even came down to jam with us, and he wrote a beautiful song that we were very excited about. After a couple weeks of these daily sessions, we made rough mixes of our ideas and bounced them down to a cassette, which was then hand delivered to Layne so he could develop his lyrical ideas. However, and quite unfortunately, Layne had slipped back into his heroin addiction, and we could not get him to come down to the studio to record a single vocal. Mark was a no show as well, his own addiction taking over his life.

The last time I saw Layne and Mark together was when I was walking into Tower Records on Mercer Street, by the Seattle Center. It was 1997, and I went there to buy some world music records for another project I was starting called Tuatara. As I walked towards the front door, I saw Layne and Mark walking out together, and they both looked to be in terrible shape. My conversation with them was brief and uncomfortable, and they clearly didn't want to talk to me about anything, much less the second Mad Season album that we had halted production on.

Sadly, Baker went first, dying from a heroin overdose on his kitchen floor in January of 1999. I was the last person to speak with him on the phone, and we were supposed to meet for breakfast the following morning. When he didn't show up at my house, I knew something was wrong. Layne followed him in death in April of 2002, again from an overdose, alone in his apartment. The soul of the band had been totally lost.

In 2013, Mike had the idea to digitize those two concert films that we had made in 1995, and release them into the new digital universe. I simultaneously emailed Mark about an idea I had. "Hey Mark, what if we finished a couple of those songs from the second Mad Season album, as a kind of tribute to Layne and Baker. Would you be interested in doing something like that?" Mark was totally in, so I found the old rough mixes of the 18 basic tracks that Brett Eliason had recorded in 1996, and I sent them off to Mark. He picked out three of the best songs, including the beautiful song Peter had written. Mark wrote lyrics and sang all three songs in a manner that was so powerful, it was like we were back in 1995, all over again. We had another successful album, a re-issue, but this time it came with three new tracks, two concert films, and a bunch of live recordings. People still remembered the magic.

Two years after that, in January of 2015, Mad Season played together one last time with some special guest singers, and the support of the Seattle Symphony. Mike had somehow made a connection with their conductor, Ludovic Morlot, who had a passion for doing symphonic reworkings of popular music. Apparently that cello part I had recorded for "River Of Deceit" was the starting point that had inspired Ludovic to write orchestrations for three Mad Season songs: "Long Gone Day," "River Of Deceit," and "I Don't Know Anything."

There we were at Seattle's Benaroya Hall, a 50-piece orchestra behind us, with me on drums, Mike on guitar, and our good friend Duff McKagan, bassist for Guns & Roses, filling in on bass. I had invited Mark to do the concert, but he wasn't able to do it because of a previous touring commitment. Instead, we decided to invite several guest vocalists to sing Layne and Mark's parts, and one of those singers happened to be the great Chris Cornell of Soundgarden, one of the most talented musicians and songwriters to ever come out of the Pacific Northwest.

One of the highlights of the night was when Alice In Chains drummer, Sean Kinney, and Soundgarden drummer, Matt Cameron, joined all of us on stage, as we played along to Layne's original 1994 vocal track for the song, "All Alone." In that moment between the three of us drummers, I could feel that we had healed the rift that had been simmering since that 1992 tour. We had all lost dear friends and band mates, our pain was mutual, and now it could be released.

A few days after the show, an email circulated between Chris Cornell, Mike McCready, Duff McKagan, and myself. The four of us had enjoyed playing together so much that Chris suggested we keep playing as some kind of new band. We agreed that we shouldn't call it Mad Season, but we all wanted to do something new, something fresh, because the musical chemistry we had just created on stage was electric. I know that all four of us were excited about that possibility, but sadly we lost Chris as well, in May of 2017. Now with Mark Lanegan's death in 2022, three of the greatest singers of my generation are gone, and all three of them had performed with Mad Season.

There are times when I just can't believe that these 3 titans are gone, and it feels like a dream that I will eventually wake from.

But when they were here, it was a beautiful dream, nonetheless.

AN AUSTRALIAN EXCURSION

In January of 1995, right in between the completion and the release of Mad Season's debut album, the Screaming Trees did a brief tour of Australia. We had been invited to play the Big Day Out festival, which was a kind of traveling festival that took a group of bands to every major city in Australia, very much akin to the Lollapalooza festival, which also used to tour around the US. With Australia, which really only has five major cites (Brisbane, Sydney, Melbourne, Adelaide, and Perth), the entire country can be toured in about 10 days, which is about the shortest and nicest national tour you can have on this planet.

My parents used to live in Sydney when my father worked for an Australian explosives company, so I had visited Australia a couple of times before the Trees ever toured there. I loved the country, loved the people, but mostly loved the landscape, which is absolutely spectacular almost everywhere you go. I was extremely stoked when the Trees announced that we would finally be touring there.

We would be playing on the main stage of the festival with bands like Hole, Ministry, and The Cult. It was actually a pretty great line up because the emphasis was on real rock & roll, and all of those bands were great live bands. Plus, the Australians are a nation of people who love rock & roll fervently.

I was particularly happy to be playing with The Cult, because their early albums, specifically *Love* (1985) and *Electric* (1987) were some of the best rock albums made in the 1980s. I had those albums in college, right beside my John Coltrane and Miles Davis albums.

We became somewhat chummy with Ian Astbury, the uniquely talented vocalist of The Cult, and once, when we were hanging out in the lobby of our hotel, I saw Ian and Gary Lee having a conversation where they were laughing jovially between themselves. I couldn't hear what was being said, but when Lee turned to leave to get on the tour bus, Ian slapped him on his large backside and declared, "Lee, you naughty boy!" I heard the last part and laughed out loud, because number one, Lee was not naughty, and number two, I'd never seen anyone slap Lee's huge ass, much less a famous rocker like Ian Astbury. This was going to be a great tour.

Near the beginning, we had a day off in Brisbane, and having been in that city before, I knew that there was a huge rainforest just inland from the ocean. I told the boys in the band and the crew that I was taking them on a forced march through the rainforest the next day. I rented a minivan from the hotel, which I drove myself, hauling the band and crew to the trail head. Mark did not join us, but the Conner brothers and most of our crew did. It was a great day, and on the hike we saw numerous exotic birds and even some wild Koala sitting in the eucalyptus trees, which was extremely rare.

After we returned to our hotel later that evening, I found that I had been upgraded to a much nicer room on the top floor overlooking the ocean. I think it was because I had rented that expensive van through the hotel's concierge. I invited Van to come up and share a bottle of wine that had been left in my room, and we sat on the balcony and watched the light play over the ocean as the sun went down. We talked and laughed about our insane band, our relationships at home, and what the future might hold for us. That was one of the best memories I have of my time in the Trees, adventuring around Australia, and becoming much better friends along the way.

Before we embarked on this Australian tour, there was talk of us playing a few shows in Japan, which because of its proximity to Australia, could happen right after the Australian tour wrapped up. The plan was that we would fly from Sydney to Tokyo and play a handful of shows around Japan. The problem that emerged was Mark's now-enormous heroin habit.

On the Australian tour, Mark was doing this drug constantly, especially because of the junkie camaraderie he had developed with other musicians, and various mucky mucks on the tour. There were times when we entered our dressing room to witness some combination of debauchery, some of it with complete strangers, and we would see blood on the ceiling where one or more of them had fired their syringe into the air like a gun, an absurdly ridiculous practice that junkies do to "mark their spot." It was unbelievably gross, and it radically contrasted to what was generally a pretty amazing tour in a stunningly beautiful country.

As the Australian shows were winding down, our tour manager told us that there was no realistic way we could get into Japan, largely because Mark looked absolutely terrible, and Japanese customs probably wouldn't even let him pass through. Also, and perhaps more importantly, heroin was not readily available in Japan like it was in the US, Europe, and Australia, so Mark would be terribly sick from withdrawals the entire time we were there. If he did try to score heroin in Japan, he would most certainly go to jail or even prison, because the Japanese don't mess around with drug addicts.

Thus, the Australian tour wrapped up, the Japan tour was canceled, and the Trees headed home. For me, at least that meant I was returning to a new home—a 1925 Craftsman bungalow that I had recently bought with my advance from the Mad Season album. It was a house very much like the kind I used to work on when I worked for that Seattle construction company. It was modest, but cool and sturdily built, like they used to build them in the old days. I finally owned my own home, and even though the Green Lake house had yielded some wonderful times and many great songs, it was now time for me to finally start my own life that music had bought for me.

I didn't know what would be happening with the Trees in the future, as there was still no timetable for us to record our next album. On top of that, Mark was in really terrible shape. We had the Mad Season album soon to be released, and I was about to start a new project called Tuatara, with Justin Harwood of Luna, and Peter Buck of R.E.M., but everything was totally up in the air and nothing had materialized. Thus, I spent the next few months remodeling and fixing up my old bungalow.

Because sometimes, just working with your hands is enough to settle the soul.

HELLO, I'M JOHNNY CASH

It had now been six months since the recording of the Mad Season album, which was also when Mark heard me playing the upright bass for the song, "Long Gone Day." He said to me at the time that he had no idea I even played upright bass, and that I should play it on some Screaming Trees songs. We did exactly that, and I played upright bass on a couple B-Sides that we recorded, including the gospel classic, "Peace In The Valley," and an acoustic version of "Winter Song." Additionally, I had sparked a friendship with Mike Johnson, the bassist of Dinosaur Jr., who was also Mark's guitarist on his solo albums. Mike was making his own solo album, and he needed an upright bassist for his debut offering, *A Year Of Mondays* (1996).

I wasn't really sure how Mark was doing because after the Australian tour and the two Mad Season shows we played together, I never saw him very much. So I was surprised when he called me out of the blue and asked me to play upright bass in his solo band. I was shocked actually, because I didn't think Mark was ever going to play a solo show at all, but indeed, he had booked two of them in Seattle and Portland—opening for the legendary Johnny Cash.

Wow, I had never even considered that possibility in my mind. Maybe Mark was on the upswing?

This was the very first incarnation of the Mark Lanegan Band, and it also included Dan Peters of Mudhoney on drums, Mike Johnson on guitar, Jay Mascis of Dinosaur Jr. on additional guitar, and a violinist named Dave Krueger. It was a real supergroup of great talent, and a wonderful group of guys to play with.

This was one of those once in a lifetime opportunities that probably wouldn't happen again. I mean, I grew up listening to my dad's Johnny Cash albums, and seeing him on TV when he had his own variety show in the 1970s. Johnny was already a global legend by the time these shows were announced, which was in September of 1995. That made Mr. Cash 63 years old at the time, which was only 5 years older than Mark was at the time of his death, and only 8 years older than I am as I write this story. I think about that now, with my own age and the passage of time, and how these icons of music are now gone and very few seem capable of filling their shoes.

As the shows neared, Mark was probably thinking about these same things, and although it's impossible to compare these two men to each other, the pairing was metaphoric. Many saw Mark as a kind of Generation X version of Johnny Cash, because both singers had booming baritones, and a propensity to live on life's edge while writing great songs about it.

We rehearsed for the shows in my Craftsman bungalow, because I had now built a small studio in the basement. I had also bought a new coat for the show, one of those long suede coats, which I thought looked more country than rock. Mark laughed when I put it on, saying I looked like his high school math teacher, but I wore it anyway.

When it came time to play the Seattle show, Mr. Cash stood on the side of the stage while we played a short set of Mark's excellent songs, taken from his first two solo albums, *The Winding Sheet (1990)* and *Whiskey For The Holy Ghost (1994)*, both of which had been released on Sub Pop. There was of course a heckler in the audience, because there will always be knuckleheads who shout from the safety of darkness, but Mark shut him down with a few choice words, "Hey man, I don't come down to 7-11 and harass you at your job," and the audience cheered. The show went great, as expected, and then we waited for Johnny Cash to play.

"Hello, I'm Johnny Cash" was his usual opening statement and the crowd roared to its feet. The hits played on and on, and halfway through the set his wife, June Carter, came out to do their famous duets.

The thing I remembered the most, besides watching Johnny in person, was his original drummer, W. S. Holland, who played a ridiculously huge, white sparkle, double kick drum set with multiple tom toms—most which he never played. I suppose that's because

Johnny's sound was always a more simple affair—a kick drum (one, and only one), a snare drum, and a hi-hat. Occasionally there might be a ride cymbal, but W. S. Holland rocked that giant drum set regardless, his perfectly pompadoured silver hair, reflecting the stage lights like a mirror ball.

That original Mark Lanegan Band never played together again, as our individual paths continued in different directions. Mark did ask me to play upright bass, drums, and vibraphone on a couple of his future solo albums, those being, *I'll Take Care Of You (1999)*, and *Imitations (2013)*. But I always acknowledge that it was Mark who saw my musical potential beyond the Screaming Trees, and that is why we were able to collaborate in Mad Season, on his solo albums, and on other projects over the decades.

Very few people alive today can say that they opened for Johnny Cash. But I can—because of Mark Lanegan.

DUST

With the release of Mark's brilliant second solo album, *Whiskey For The Holy Ghost* (1994), and the release of the Mad Season album the following year (1995), Mark said something to me that I think was very prophetic. He thought that by making two commercially successful albums back to back with *Sweet Oblivion* and *Above,* the Screaming Trees had a much better chance of redeeming ourselves in our bid to make another album. The aborted album from 1994 had sort of been forgotten, and we probably had enough momentum to get a new budget approved from Epic Records, so we could finally make the record the Trees knew we could make.

In hindsight, I think Mark was exactly right about the first part. He and I had created great momentum with our respective albums, and we were certainly back in the game as individual artists. But the fact remained that the Trees, unlike Mad Season, had still not done as well commercially as other Seattle bands had done in that same period of time. I still believed that our label would be involved with everything we did, no matter what our "critical acclaim" was, but I suppose that is the trade off for being on a major label. If you're on a corporate label, the suits will always have their fingers in the pie.

It had now been a full year since the aborted album sessions, Mad Season had only played those two official concerts, and Mark had done very little promotion for his second solo album—those Johnny Cash shows were about all he did. I was now starting to run out money again, because I had used all of my Mad Season advance to buy my house, and I was still in the middle of remodeling it. Plus, the Trees only payed me when we were on the road earning money. I had a mortgage to pay every month, including all the other expenses that come with homeownership. Incredibly, I was actually thinking about returning to my old construction job, building homes and maybe going back to school to study architecture. There were just all these roadblocks every time our attention returned to the Screaming Trees.

I brought this up with the Trees accountant and this got back to Mark, who called me with a desperate tone in his voice, "Please don't go back to construction bro, I'm worried you'll cut off your fingers like Tony Iommi did." (Tony Iommi, the genius guitarist of Black Sabbath, had infamously cut off the tips of a couple of his fingers on the last day of his job at a metal factory, right when Black Sabbath got signed to a major label.)

The accountant assured me that the Trees were definitely going to make another album and that I'd get paid again, and just to hang in there for a bit longer. And so I did, living on a shoestring budget, in a half-finished house remodel, in the hopes that the Trees would get our album budget approved.

Our old reliable A&R rep, Bob Pfeifer, had recently left Epic to start a new job as the president of Disney's label, Hollywood Records, so the Trees were assigned a new A&R. He was a young wunderkind named Michael Goldstone, who had signed Pearl Jam, Rage Against The Machine, and a few other bands that were actually quite good. Michael was going to oversee our next album and we liked him because he was a quiet, reasonable guy who knew a lot about music. We also had a new manager now, or rather two of them—the titans of music management, Q Prime, spearheaded by their two founders, Peter Mensch and Cliff Bernstein. Between Q Prime and Michael Goldstone, we had a very strong team, indeed it was a kind of dream team, and they were ready to guide us through the process of making the Trees seventh album.

Lee was still writing songs at the Green Lake house using his old Tascam four-track recorder, which made astoundingly great sounding demos. Van was doing the same at his new house using a similar machine, and I had set up a small studio in the basement of my bungalow where I worked on my own songs. We would all send our songs over to Lee on cassette tapes, which he would then make into compilation tapes for Mark. Mark would then pick out the songs he liked for us to further develop.

I remember talking a lot with Lee during this period of time, asking him for more songwriting tips, and during a subsequent conversation we had for this book, he referred to this period of time as "songwriting jail." This was because Mark was calling him every day for new songs, which made Lee furiously write a group of songs, put them on a cassette, and then drive it over to Mark's apartment on Capitol Hill, making sure to stop at *Jack In The Box* along the way to bring Mark his requested dinner. Lee was literally working every day of his life, writing songs for our next album, and doing an early version of *Door Dash* for Mark.

We also decided to re-record a few of the best songs we had attempted during the aborted album sessions a year earlier, so with those handful of great songs, combined with all the new songs we had all written together, we felt like we finally had enough material to make a truly great album. Lee made a final compilation cassette that had the best of the best songs that Mark had approved, and he sent one cassette to Michael Goldstone at Epic, and one cassette to Peter and Cliff at Q Prime. Then we waited.

It reminded me of a time when Bob Pfeifer was still our A&R at Epic, and he said something that I will never forget: "Epic Records can afford to make Screaming Trees records because the label is making Michael Jackson money." Michael Jackson was also signed to Epic Records, and Bob then added, "But the Screaming Trees make Epic Records look much cooler than they are, because the Trees are outlaws who can't be controlled, and that helps the label sign more bands who want to be like the Screaming Trees."

Oh man, if those bands only knew what that were in for....

I always remembered Bob's words, and the financial truth about the pecking order at record labels because it's gospel truth. The big stars earn the big money, which in turn helps the up and coming bands become stars themselves. And maybe that's why Epic agreed to fund another album for the Screaming Trees, and they even increased our budget beyond what our contract said. I guess I wasn't going to have to go back to house building after all.

This time we decided to go with a totally different producer, and we picked a large and jovial gentleman named, George Drakoulias. George had produced some of our favorite albums over the previous years for bands like the Jayhawks and their superb, *Hollywood Town Hall* (1992), as well as a couple of the early Black Crowes albums.

George had been a kind of protégé of the producer Rick Rubin, although George had much more of a hands on approach to his producing because he had engineering skills as well. We met George and we liked him immediately, and since we all wanted to get out of Seattle, we made a plan to record in sunny Los Angeles.

We flew to LA in the fall of 1995, and we stayed at one of those corporate residency apartment-hotels in Burbank. The rehearsals that George had lined up for us were located in a large and very loud rehearsal studio in Hollywood, where our room was nestled between the space where Rage Against The Machine rehearsed, and the other side was a band called The Wallflowers. It was loud as hell to say the least, and maybe that was a good thing because we played even louder so that we could hear ourselves.

The most important factor in these rehearsals, which I picked up on immediately, was that George got us to become hyper-focus on our arrangements, which left very little room for jamming or noodling around. George wanted the songs to be as tight and concise as possible, and we automatically merged with this approach. It was essentially what we had done for the songs on *Sweet Oblivion*, but we had somehow forgotten that method in the ensuing years. It was in my blood as a drummer and arranger to think this way, so I carried this same philosophy forward in my own work as a producer.

We rehearsed diligently for about three weeks, refining the songs exactly as we had done for *Sweet Oblivion*, except instead of being in a cold, wet Seattle winter, we were now in sunny, warm LA. This process made our songs become extremely tight and focused, like small musical explosives where the verses were set, the choruses were big and melodious, and we came up with really interesting intros and outros, which was really my musical contribution to the songs, tying them together as a body of work.

George's main advice to me as we prepared to record the basic tracks was, "You gotta make me dance." George didn't want me playing to sterile click tracks, but he did make these really interesting loops of famous drummers like John Bonham, Clyde Stubblefield, and other classic beat masters, which created a naturally groovy, dance quality to the rhythms. Those rhythmic loops are what I would play along with in my headphones, as we perfected the arrangements and tempos for the songs.

By the time we finally set up to record the basic tracks in the gigantic *Frank Sinatra Studio* in the basement of Capital Records in Central Hollywood, we were totally ready. George would play his drum loops until I had the grooves embedded in my body, and that's when we'd start recording a basic track. I specifically focused on making George stand up and dance behind the console in the control room, because I knew if I could see George dancing, I knew I was in the zone.

George's main engineer at the time was the well-known, Jim Scott, who had worked on numerous classic rock albums, won Grammys, and always arrived at the studio in one of his many 1960s muscle cars, of which one was a classic Pontiac GTO. Somehow seeing Jim drive up every morning in that bad ass muscle car, his shoulder length silver hair blowing in the wind, inspired me in my own playing. We were making a rock album after all, and Jim's superb engineering and technical abilities certainly put some sparkle on it—he captured the power of the Trees in our fighting form best.

I should also mention that Jim's muscle car arrivals were comedically offset by George's daily arrival in his British Mini Cooper, which in 1995 was an extremely tiny car, long before the modern Mini Cooper had been upgraded to larger American standards. George's Mini Cooper was so small that when he got out of it, we were surprise to see that the car held him at all, being that George was a very large man.

George also wanted the Trees to enjoy life a little more, beyond the poverty level existence we had all been living under. He took us to great Jewish delis for enormous pastrami sandwiches, and swanky restaurants for dinner where the "big time smarty pants" of Hollywood hung out, as George called them. He even got a few of the band members to start smoking cigars, which are not the sort of thing I associate with enjoying life more. Yet when I think about recording that album with George, the smell of cigar smoke seems to linger in my memory.

All of those things, combined with George's dance requirement in my drumming, made our new basic tracks swing like no other album I had done up to that point. The battleship swing that Van and I had been perfecting on the road was finally back, captured on tape.

We recorded all of the basic tracks in Frank Sinatra's famous room in less than a week, with Van fixing his bass lines from behind the console right after my drum takes were selected. After we had the rhythm tracks done, we moved over to *Sunset Sound*, another classic studio in central

Hollywood. There, Lee finished his guitar tracks, which also included the use of more interesting and exotic stringed instruments, like the electric sitar he used for the song, "Halo Of Ashes."

I was also given more license with my own overdub ideas, rather than just being limited to playing the occasional tambourine or shaker. With the Mad Season songs, I had been trying out new percussion sounds, and Mark encouraged me to do this again on the Trees songs. I had also written an intro and an outro for the song, "Gospel Plow," which had me playing an Indian harmonium and a set of tablas, which set the mood for a more exotic sound. I also played African drums and congas on the songs, "Halo Of Ashes," "Make My Mind," and "Dime Western." There was even space for a cello part here and there, and since I had played cello in Mad Season, I was able to recreate the same affect in a few spots. All of these new and sometimes exotic instruments made our album sound extremely lush and adventurous, and very different from anything the Trees had done before.

Mark was in a much better mood as well, and his lead vocals were sounding more inspired and quite beautiful. I think it was largely because he was in sunny Hollywood, and away from the gritty, druggy Seattle we had all grown tired of. He also had a new girlfriend in Selene Vigil, who was the singer of a Seattle Riot Grrrl band called, Seven Year Bitch. Selene was beautiful, talented, and super cool, and she easily hung out with the rough and rowdy Screaming Trees. Everything was flowing perfectly, and there was peace between us all.

When it came time to do the backing vocals, Lee, Van, and I would often sing together, which gave us a much more unified vocal sound. Some special guests stopped by too, like Chris Goss, lead singer of one of our favorite bands, The Masters Of Reality, and this added another beautiful voice to the palate.

As we neared the end of the final overdubs, George brought in a couple of *ringers* (ace musicians) who added some final magic to our album. One was Mike McCready of Pearl Jam and Mad Season, who recorded the absolutely ripping guitar solo on the song, "Dying Days." Then we got what was perhaps the most impressive musical contribution on the entire album from Benmont Tench, the keyboardist for Tom Petty and the Heartbreakers. Benmont was a friend of George's, and he recorded some truly virtuosic, scene-stealing keyboard parts on our songs, which gave the album a flair of genius that we didn't expect.

By this time, we were pretty much done with the album, but there were still a few small tweaks that our A&R, Michael Goldstone, wanted us to make. This time we decided to go back to New York City, because Andy Wallace was going to mix our album again, plus everyone on our team—Q-Prime, Michael Goldstone, and Epic Records were all in New York City.

George chose *The Hit Factory* for our final "fixing session," and it was there that I re-recorded the drum track for the song, "Look At You." This was because the label was thinking about making it a single, and they had deemed that the original tempo was just too slow for radio. I came up with the idea of playing the drums in double time, with the addition of overdubbed drum fills, the way Ringo Starr did them on Beatles albums. The label loved the revised version of the song, so the album was officially declared finished and sent off to Andy Wallace to do his mixes.

Mark is the one who came up with the album's title, *Dust*, because we all felt like we had worked so hard as a band, that we had indeed become dust itself. It was Van's new brother in-lawn, a painter named Mark Danielson, who imagined what *Dust* might look like on canvas, and that's how we ended up with the spooky, ethereal album cover.

Mark asked me and Van to oversee the mastering again with Howie Weinberg, who mastered the album loud as hell, just as he had done for *Sweet Oblivion*. This time I left his mastering lab with a CD in my hand—not a cassette, we were in the digital age now, so I could listen and approve the final master. I passed the same CD on to my good friend Peter Buck, guitarist of R.E.M., who was in the middle of an incredible run of back-to-back album successes. I wanted his honest opinion on what we had just created because I was too close to the all-consuming process. The next day Peter called me at home and exclaimed:

"This is the heaviest gospel album ever made—I fucking love it!"

HAVE YOURSELF A BUD

As the band steadied itself for the expected world tour that would start when *Dust* was released, I focused on wrapping up a new project that I had started during the downtime between the Mad Season *Above* album in 1994, and the soon to be released *Dust* album in 1996.

I had started an instrumental, soundtrack project called Tuatara, which included Peter Buck, Justin Harwood from the band Luna, and the mono-named Skerik, who had played those beautiful sax solos on Mad Season's, "Long Gone Day." I financed the project myself and managed to get the first Tuatara album, *Breaking The Ethers (1997)*, recorded and mixed on a shoestring budget, which was my first foray into making albums where I was the main producer. I presented the album to the new president of Epic Records, Richard Griffiths, who was British and seemed to have a keener, more sophisticated musical appreciation than anyone else we had worked with at Sony. I thought Richard would appreciate some of my own musical ideas, and as it turned out, he really liked Tuatara. The next thing I heard from our attorney was that I had an offer from Epic Records to sign Tuatara directly to the label, as a separate band not affiliated with the Screaming Trees.

Simultaneously, the Trees were asked to play on the 1996 Lollapalooza festival, which would include several shows around the US. These shows would feature Metallica as the headliner, but there were some far more interesting bands that were also playing on the tour including Soundgarden (my all-time favorite band of that era), Devo, the Ramones, and several other very interesting musical acts.

The Trees were set to play second on the bill, so our shows were always early in the day when people were still arriving at the festival, and the blazing hot sun sucked much of the life out of the opening bands. It was not a good time slot to play on any festival, but at the time, Lollapalooza was still considered to be the best music festival in the United States.

Fortunately, the Trees had made the decision to add a second rhythm guitarist to our line up, which allowed Lee to focus on the more demanding guitar leads that he had recorded on *Dust*. That rhythm guitarist was the now world famous, Joshua Homme, formerly of the desert rock band Kyuss, who had yet to form his next band, Queens Of The Stone Age. Josh was an awesome addition to the Trees, in that he played rhythm guitar extremely well, and his pot smoking, velour shirt wearing persona turned out to be the best addition the Trees could have made.

Josh also recommended a new front of house soundman, a guy simply known as Hutch—he had done the front of house mixing for Josh's previous band, Kyuss. Between Josh and Hutch, the energy these two gentlemen brought to our band made our shows much tighter, more enjoyable, and much better sounding. I think it was because Josh was a guitar-playing version similar to me as a drummer, and Hutch was kind of a Zen monk behind the console, giving the Trees a superb sounding live show to present to the world.

The tour also had one of the oddest, but also one of the most entertaining additions to the main stage—the Shao Lin Fighting Monks of China. They had been added to perform their acrobatic martial art stunts in between the Trees and the other bands, so technically the Screaming Trees were opening for the Shaolin Fighting Monks—another Spinal Tap moment. I could relate to the monks though because of my own Kung Fu training, and we formed a language-free friendship that included the exchange of gifts and even some swords, which will appear in a later story.

By the end of the 20 dates on the 1996 Lollapalooza tour, I had become pretty good friends with the Shao Lin monks, but I had determined that the tour's musical acts had devolved into what might as well have been called The Angry White Man Tour. Every single band was made up of white guys screaming into microphones, while they bashed away through their songs. It had become the exact opposite of the cool, alternative Lollapalooza that we had come to love in the early 1990s. Again, the Trees saw no statistical bump in our sales figures, and it appeared that the entire tour was something of a wash. Even the larger music media seemed disinterested in the tour, and it was shortly after that 1996 Lollapalooza that the festival disappeared entirely. It finally re-emerged in 2005 in its current form as a stationary, multi-day festival in Chicago, which has vastly improved it's musical variety.

At some point, near the end of Lollapalooza and before we started our next tour, the Trees were offered two very different opportunities at the same time, both of which were totally left field offers, but they also came with the prospect of considerable public exposure. The first was the possibility of the Trees doing a Budweiser commercial, if we could write a song that their marketing people liked. The other offer was an opening slot for the band, Bon Jovi.

Now, the possibility of a Budweiser commercial was received as almost a joke—the Trees doing a beer commercial? Sure, we drank a lot of beer, but the Trees were not the kind of look you would want on a TV commercial. The same could be said opening for Bon Jovi.

Both ideas were presented to us by our managers, Peter and Cliff, who were two of the toughest, most hardened managers in the music business. Peter had managed AC/DC during the death of Bon Scott, and then their epic comeback album, *Back In Black (1980)*. Additionally, Peter and Cliff had been the managers of Metallica from the very beginning, taking them from an unknown band into global megastars. They also managed Courtney Love's band, Hole, as well as, bizarrely, Weird Al Yankovic, who, however absurd he was musically, apparently made a lot of money doing comedy knock-offs of other people's hit songs. We trusted that Peter and Cliff knew exactly what they were doing, so we listened to their advice very carefully. We thought, if Q-Prime can make someone as ridiculous as Weird Al Yankovic globally famous, then they certainly know how to make the Trees more successful. We started seriously thinking about doing a Budweiser commercial.

Other bands and solo artists had done beer commercials in the past, but it also made them look like total sell-outs. Or as Mark would constantly warn, "That's veering into steakhouse," which is exactly what a beer commercial is.

The other side of the argument was that the Trees had another great song, "All I Know," climbing the charts, and a beer commercial could put us over the top. To be perfectly honest, we talked about it over the next couple weeks, as we considered the ramifications of a critically acclaimed rock band doing something so blatantly commercial as a beer song, which would have obviously been for the money.

When I spoke with Gary Lee about this, he remembered that the initial offer was only $10,000, a paltry sum to sell your soul, even back then. He also remembered that the Budweiser pitchman suggested we write something similar to the chorus from our previous hit, "Nearly Lost You," which could be re-sung as, "I Nearly Lost My Bud." As dismally awful as that sounds, it actually sounded catchy, especially when Mark added a few more ridiculous lines and then ended the jingle with the tagline, "Have yourself a Bud," which made the entire bus laugh like hyenas on crack cocaine. We even developed a Budweiser songbook that had ongoing verses that were so funny, I'd laugh until I was crying and couldn't breathe. I mean, what kind of band would take such revelry in dismantling our own songs, turning them into horrible advertising jingles? Only the Screaming Trees, usually drunk, and bored out of our minds in the back of the bus.

We weighed the pros and cons of being visually identified on a TV commercial, assuming the Budweiser marketing team were actually willing to put our ugly mugs on screen. On the one hand, this would dramatically raise the profile of the band because television has a massive audience, much more than even films. On the other hand, it would be immediately uncool for us to do such a thing, which would forever tarnish our musical credibility and give us the scarlet letter of "sellouts." We obviously decided that our reputation as songwriters far outweighed any benefit we would gain from any TV commercial.

The second proposal that Peter and Cliff presented to us was the offer to open for Bon Jovi, which was still a very big band at the time, and still is to this day. Despite them being more aligned with the hair metal bands of the late 1980s, apparently Jon Bon Jovi really liked the Screaming Trees and he had specifically asked for us to be their opener on their next US tour.

I was actually open to the idea, because hell, it was now 1996, half a decade after Nirvana kicked open the door of the alternative universe, so if any rock band was still going strong, they must be doing something right. Maybe opening for Bon Jovi would be a great opportunity?

Again, the band debated opening for a band that was playing large amphitheaters that held upwards of 30,000 people. We had done that with the Spin Doctors and it was a miserable experience, and then there was the Alice In Chains tour before that. Neither tour did anything to help raise the profile of the Trees, it only served to demoralize us.

However, we did consider that playing with Bon Jovi could be different, because Jon appeared to be a cool guy with good taste, who knew a fair bit about music, which history has proven to be correct. And even though Bon Jovi were essentially glam rockers and the Trees were exactly the opposite, we figured that a certain percentage of his audience would like us and therefore we'd grow our fan base. However, the mistakes we had made as an opening band, up to and including the Lollapalooza tour, weighed heavily on us, and we ultimately decided against Mr. Bon Jovi's offer as well.

Instead, the Trees decided to lumber on, alternating between opening up for other bands, and being the occasional headliner.

But by this point, the band was on autopilot.

WARDROBE MALFUNCTIONS

Despite the general gloom that seemed to pervade the various tours that the Trees undertook between the years 1992 and 1996, there were moments of great levity and inside jokes that kept the band and crew rolling with laughter for days and weeks on end. It often started with one of the crew guys commenting on something they had witnessed the previous day or night, but more often than not, it was an impersonation or character that drum tech, John Hicks, had created. He would keep us in stitches for weeks and months at a time, with an ongoing evolution of some character he had created. I know it's hard to believe that the Trees could even laugh with the reputation we had created, but we all laughed, all the time. Laughter is how we coped with the ridiculous situations that we kept finding ourselves in, and such was the case with the incidents described below.

At some point on any given tour that a band undertakes, there comes a time when the clothing you have chosen for that tour either wears out, becomes too big or too small (depending on your food consumption or dieting habits), or the clothing becomes unwearable altogether because of a change of seasons. In the case of these next two stories, it was all of the above.

In our first example, we have guitarist Gary Lee Conner, who, like his brother Van, was a very large man who tended to wear a nearly identical outfit on stage, and off stage for that matter. This consisted of long, baggy, denim cut off shorts, a long sleeved t-shirt, and Converse Chuck Taylor tennis shoes. In addition to this, Lee also wore his ubiquitous knee braces, so as to be able to do his stage acrobatics and slides, ala Pete Townshend. Lee was quite a sight to see, and anyone who saw the Trees perform live could never forget him—he was 110% full on, for the entire duration of the show. When Lee was having a good night, he kind of stole the show from the rest of us, but when he had a bad night, well, it was a like a hurricane gone sideways.

On this particular night, we were playing at the Seattle Center Arena at one of those shows on the Alice In Chains Tour. It was the same show where Alice's production manager dropped the stage curtain right on my drum seat, so that my arms were hitting the back of the curtain. Even at our hometown of Seattle, this small-minded, butt rock harassment continued, so I was in a very bad mood from the downbeat of the first song.

We had all been losing weight on the tour as well, the result of not enough food in the catering area to offset the energy we were expending for months on end. The sheer caloric burn of a single Screaming Trees show could make me lose 10 pounds in a single night, and even the Conner brothers were dropping weight like a bride before her wedding day.

This is because the Trees live show was modeled after a cluster of bands known for their live wire performances: The MC5, The Stooges, The Who, and Black Flag. These were our musical heroes, so the Trees played like those bands, full tilt from the beginning of the show, to the very end. There were no long pauses between songs, and no quarter given to audience members who harassed us. Indeed, Mark had a reputation for jumping off the stage multiple times over the years in pursuit of a doomed heckler. This kind of job makes you lose weight, a lot of it.

At this particular Seattle show, Lee was in the middle of a series of successive windmills, a move that he stole directly from Pete Townshend. But if you've ever seen vintage footage of Pete Townsend doing windmills, versus Gary Lee Conner, it's pretty clear that Gary Lee wins the windmill contest. On this night, Lee was whipping up a sonic storm and that's when, unexpectedly, Lee's oversized denim shorts with boxer shorts included, dropped to his ankles, mid-windmill. All that was left behind was Lee's actual, bare behind. Fortunately there was a guitar hanging in front of him.

It was the same huge ass that Ian Astbury of The Cult would slap with a laugh, in that Australian hotel lobby a couple years later.

This is the only time I ever saw Mark completely double over on stage, he was howling. I was laughing hard too, as I tried to keep the beat going to whatever song we were playing, which was an impossible task. I mean, I was *behind* Lee, so I saw it all.

Van was howling too, Mark was practically crying, and even Lee started to laugh in that uncomfortable realization that your pants are down around your ankles, in front of several thousand people, in your hometown. Finally Mark managed to squeak out, "Pull up your pants, boy!"

Lee did the exact opposite, in fact he stepped out of the fallen cut off shorts (thank god he hiked up his boxers first), and picked up the shorts, whirling them around his head like a vaudevillian stripper, and then let them fly off the stage. It was unlike anything I'd ever seen Lee do, before or since, and as our show continued, I forgot all about the god damn stage curtain that was sitting on my shoulders.

The second "disrobing event" happened near the end of an excruciatingly hot show on the 1996 Lollapalooza tour. We were playing somewhere in the Midwest, at one of those god-forsaken speedway tracks that serves as a show grounds. It was a miserable, hot, humid, and utterly depressing shit hole, the kind of place where Kid Rock or Ted Nugent would have thrived.

Midway through our opening set in the blazing hot sun, Mark suddenly and unexpectedly began to remove his clothes. This was a startling event in and of itself, because on the 1996 tour, Mark had changed his clothing and hairstyle pretty dramatically, looking more glam than grunge. He had cut his hair to shoulder length, and it seemed more blonde than his usual red. He also painted his nails black, and was wearing cool fabric shirts rather than the ubiquitous flannel, and he often wore colorful pants that were either bright red or yellow. He actually looked great, the best I had ever seen him, and we all liked this new version of Mark.

The first article of clothing to come off that day were Mark's trademark Doc Martens, which he unlaced and kicked off to the side of the stage. OK, boots are hot in this kind of weather, I thought to myself as I kept the beats going.

Next came the socks, removed in a clumsy striptease, and this was something that I had never seen before—Mark's bare feet. I hadn't even seen this on the bus and I wanted to unsee it, but now I couldn't. This left me feeling unnerved.

Lastly, Mark removed his red pants, which he wore more than any other pair and badly needed washing anyway. He was now down to his boxer shorts and a long sleeved, black, button down shirt. Thank god he didn't take off his shirt.

As our set ended, Mark sauntered off the stage as if nothing out of the ordinary had happened, and he retired to the dressing room.

I have no idea what happened to his clothes, but Mark didn't seem to want them anyway.

THE SAMURAI BASSIST

Van Conner was one of the greatest bassists I have ever played with, and that includes some other bass titans that I have recorded and toured with over the decades, including Duff McKagan of Guns & Roses, and Mike Mills of R.E.M. This is not to mention some of the outstanding session bassists that I have made albums with, but Van Conner was simply one of the best at both recording and live performance.

Born Van Patrick Conner on Saint Patrick's Day, March 17th, 1967, I attribute his musical skills to a combination of his deep knowledge of American and European popular music, in tandem with his large, bear-like physique, which, like the jazz legend Charles Mingus, made bass playing the only obvious instrument for a man of such stature. All of this gave Van a melodic, yet heavy, deep swinging way of playing his instrument. Together, he and I created a rhythm section similar to the two Johns of Led Zeppelin, and Bill Ward and Geezer Butler of Black Sabbath. Both of those bands had a heavy influence on the Trees, and we honored them by referencing their styles without ever directly copying them.

Van and I made the Trees groove with that battleship swing I've mentioned a couple of times, because it bears repeating. His bass lines had the unique ability to weave together both the feel of the rhythm section and the melody of the song, which is no easy task. This is also why he was a great songwriter, and Van would often pull musical rabbits out of his hat and blow us all away with a totally original song.

Van almost always held court after our shows, with a beer in one hand and a cigarette in the other, as he chatted and told stories with our fans. He exuded a kind of Shakespearean Falstaff mystique—that of the rotund, jovial man who could talk equally about music, while delivering quick-witted repartees to the people who surrounded him. I found myself in Van's circle many a night after our shows, and during the meet and greets with fans and journalists. It was a nice way to end the evening, with laughs and some good-hearted banter before we all got back on the tour bus and drove away into the night. Despite all the ups and downs of our various tours, I always looked forward to playing with Van because he always did something to make the shows memorable, which is why this next story is dedicated to the great, gentle giant.

In late August of 1996, we had just started a short run of dates opening for the English band, Oasis. The tour also had a fantastic Welsh band, The Manic Street Preachers, as the opening act, with the Trees in the middle, and Oasis as the headliner. The Preachers and the Trees liked each other immediately, and both bands were going over fairly well with the American audiences. Oasis, on the other hand, seemed to be stumbling. Lee and I both agreed that some of the Oasis songs were pretty great, we liked their first couple albums, and Lee had even struck up a kind of songwriters friendship with Noel Gallagher, the main songwriter and guitarist for Oasis.

The Oasis guys seemed friendly enough, but there was something missing in the way they played live. The exceedingly boring "shoegazing" approach to their live show was uninteresting and peculiar to what otherwise should have been a rip-roaring concert. For whatever reason, their shows seemed to lack any real conviction, and the American audiences could feel that. That's why when you play rock & roll, you have to really believe in what you're doing and give it your all, because the audience can always tell if you don't.

Then there was the much-publicized incident where Mark and Liam Gallagher, Oasis' singer, got into some kind of verbal kerfuffle in the catering area backstage. I did not witness the incident, but I heard about it immediately afterwards when Mark told us that Liam had threatened to, "put him through the wall."

Apparently Liam had started the row by saying something to Mark about our band being called, "The Howling Branches," which was really just a bad pun on the Screaming Trees name. Maybe Liam was trying to break the ice with Mark by using a bad joke, or maybe Liam really was a jerk trying to start something. I really don't know, as I never had any interaction with Liam, aside from the one time when we were standing in the catering line, and I commented that the food was pretty good that day and he agreed. He appeared to be very polite and thankful to the kitchen staff, and he seemed like a pleasant enough fellow to me.

Mark was also in pretty bad physical shape back then from his years of heroin abuse, and this could made even the smallest of jokes go sideways. There was also the elephant in the room that the Trees had a reputation for serious brawling and fistfights, and there was a similar history with Oasis, so an unspoken challenge existed between the two surly singers. In any case, nothing ever happened between our two bands, and as they saying goes, there's Mark's side of the story, there's Liam's side, and then there's the truth.

Regardless of that absurd episode in an otherwise uneventful tour, there was one Oasis show that happened to be at a festival in Ontario, Canada where all of our bands would be opening for Neil Young and Crazy Horse. Another band on the bill included the exceptionally cool and highly original group, Spiritualized. Festivals in the 1990s seemed to take all comers, both the good and the bad I suppose, but that just added to the variety of music for all tastes.

I remember that the Trees were really looking forward to the show because we were all massive Neil Young fans, largely because Neil was a songwriter first and foremost, and anything he wrote got our attention. On this particular show, he was going to play with his old band, Crazy Horse, which he rarely toured with, thus, we were extremely honored to be one of the opening bands.

The main problem that arose on this particular day was that, once again, one of the Trees had gotten extremely wasted the night before the show, and in this case it was Van Conner. Now to be fair, Van and I had both developed serious drinking problems at about the same time, and even Lee had started drinking a little, developing a cocktail he had accidentally stumbled upon by mixing Vodka with Dr. Pepper. He named it, "2,000 Flushes," after the toilet cleaner. However, at this point in my tenure with the Trees, I was finally sober and I stayed sober for the duration of my time in the band. Mad Season had started the process, but it was also because I had seen so much depravity with drugs and alcohol with all the other bands we had toured with, that I just decided I wasn't going to be the alcoholic drummer anymore.

For some reason, unknown to anyone but him, Van had been on a real bender. He was not in very good physical shape either, so that by the time our tour manager, Danny Baird, found him passed out in his hotel room, our bus was ready to leave for the Neil Young show. As Van stumbled onto the bus, he was still in nearly blackout condition and I had a very bad feeling about it, but I hoped he might sober up enough to play our early evening set.

We rolled towards the gig, going through Canadian customs at the border, which miraculously was not the complicated ordeal it usually was. We then headed towards the festival grounds at Molson Park, which seemed to hold upwards of 50,000 people, where we found the backstage area and, as per our usual habit, headed straight towards the catering area to get some dinner. Van remained sleeping, or rather, passed out in his bunk.

To provide some context for the next stage of this epic saga, a couple weeks before we started the Oasis tour, I had purchased a set of Samurai swords at a sword shop in Philadelphia. I kept them with the Chinese swords that the Shao Lin Monks had given me on the Lollapalooza tour, and this was mainly because I had been taking sword lessons in between our tours, which was part of my newly acquired sobriety practice.

This set of swords were not the ornamental type you see in novelty shops at the local mall—these were real swords with live blades, meaning, the blades were very sharp. They were big, long, heavy swords, a Katana and a Wakizashi, which I had tucked in the space between my bunk mattress and the wall. Everyone on the bus knew they were there, and no one dared touch them. No one that is, except Van Conner, the Samurai-bassist of the Screaming Trees.

I was in catering when the story broke, like a buzz going through the room about a shocking event that was unfolding in real time. That event was Van, who was now loose backstage with a large sword that he was swinging around like a madman. Van was 6'3" and weighed about 350 pounds, so no one was going to try and disarm him. I was the only one who could—they were my swords after all. I ran out into the main courtyard and there he was, wearing black sunglasses and swinging the large Katana like a Yakuza gangster. The sunglasses hid the craziness in his eyes, but when he saw me walking towards him, his face changed to a giant smile—he knew he'd been caught.

A small crowd had gathered as I said, "Van, give me the sword, you're scaring everybody." "I'm sorry," he said, grinning as he pretended to surrender the blade to me. That's when he did the most bizarre maneuver, something I have never seen in any sword training. Van was holding the sword backwards with the blade facing him, rather than in the correct *away* position. And as he swung the sword in a large elliptic orbit, the blade passed over his left ear, nicking it and causing it to bleed. Fortunately he did not cut off his own ear, but he damn near did, and that's when I yelled out, "God damn it Van, give me that fucking sword!"

Finally he relented, and I grabbed the sword out of his hands, placing it behind my back and saying, "Van, you've got to sober up man, we have a big show to play in a couple hours opening for Neil Young!" "OK, OK," he said, as he lumbered off in no particular direction.

I returned the sword back to my bunk and hid it well under the mattress, and I went back to catering to finish my truncated and now cold dinner. Van was nowhere to be seen, apparently continuing his exploits elsewhere. I knew I had to be my brother's keeper, especially with Van, my very good friend, but I was also tired and burned out myself. The last thing I wanted to do was manage Van in the state he was in—that's the tour manager's job.

I was also concerned because Neil Young's children were backstage and we didn't want a sword-wielding giant terrorizing them. Neil's roadies had set up a kiddie pool for them and it was full of water, but only about 12 inches deep, so no sober adult would ever consider going into it. No adult except Van Conner, who was now frolicking in the kiddie pool. However to say "Van was in the pool" is not exactly the way I would describe the scene, because it was more like Van had demolished the pool, falling halfway onto the plastic edge, crushing it completely, and now the water was rushing out all around the fallen Cyclops. I waded through the soggy grass and pulled him to his feet.

"Jesus Christ Van, that pool was for Neil's kids!" I screamed. "Get out of here now before they arrest you, and get ready for the gig—we're on in an hour!"

Our set time was now upon us and I was ready and warmed up, as were Lee and Mark. Van showed up last on the side of the festival stage assisted by Danny Baird, and it was not looking good.

We started our set, and it was rocky from the get go. Van was just totally out of it and not remotely coherent in his playing. At one point about two songs in, I saw him look at me directly in the eyes and he had that same shit-eating grin as when I disarmed the sword from him. Then I saw his eyes go black, his spirit was gone, and his huge frame began to teeter. He then stopped moving entirely, dead still, and he started to tip towards me like an enormous Sequoia that had been cut off at its base and was about to make its final crash to Earth. His bass guitar was perpendicular to his body like an oversized Crusader cross, and the entire mass was coming straight down on me as vengeance.

Van landed right on top of me, his bass guitar hitting my hi-hat, snare, and rack tom in the first collision, and then he demolished the other half of my drum set as he rolled over the top of me. It was like being under that refrigerator in Cincinnati all over again. Miraculously neither of us was hurt, but I was unable to keep playing until John Hicks hurriedly reassembled my drum set mid-song, and I jumped back on.

Van eventually got back on his feet, and he pretended to play bass for the rest of our set, but by this time, Hutch had totally removed his sound from the mix—it was just too bad to make the audience listen to it.

These are the things that can happen to a man when he has spent too much time away from his family and loved ones. It was not unlike my war paint episode at the truck stop, or any of Mark's various escapades.

Van had finally reached his breaking point, and we all knew it was time to go home.

ACT III

REDEMPTION

ON THE RIVER THAMES

It was now November of 1996, and the Trees were back in Europe for what would be the very last tour we would ever play on that continent. It was a disconcerting time because despite all of the ups and downs of the previous years, we were still this critically acclaimed rock band with fans all over the world. *Rolling Stone Magazine* had picked the Trees as their "hot band of the year" for their 1996 *Hot Issue*, which also had the young actress, Cameron Diaz, on the cover—she was their "hot actress".

It was also near the end of the year, so music critics were making their year-end lists, many of them writing that *Dust* was the best rock album of the year. The Trees were also invited to play on a few European TV shows, including *Later with Jools Holland,* a really cool British TV show that featured the best bands in the world. The Trees played that show, performing two songs from *Dust,* the songs, "Halo Of Ashes," and, "All I Know," which we played surprisingly well, considering it was television. These performances can still be viewed online, and although they are sonically pretty good, it is visually apparent that the band is exhausted, and Mark in particular looks like he is barely hanging on.

Throughout the remainder of the European tour, we played our own headline shows, most of which were in England, Scotland, and northern Europe. We tended to play most of our shows in either Germany or the UK, as those were the two biggest music markets in Europe, and to be fair, we had some truly great shows on that tour, like our sold out show at the now demolished, London Astoria.

It was the day before that show in London when Mark suggested that he and I go CD shopping. He wanted to look for some rare British folk albums that were not available in the US, but might be found in some of the more eccentric music stores in London, the most eccentric city in the world. I think Mark might have been doing research for his next solo album because obscure folk artists were his go-to music when he was in a creative mood. It was also a sunny day in London and uncharacteristically warm, so off we went to go album hunting.

We spent the early afternoon looking through various shops, and I think Mark must have spent well over a thousand British pounds on CDs, because he had a very large plastic bag full of them, some apparently quite rare. At one point on our journey, we realized that we were right at the edge of the River Thames, which snakes through London on its way back way to the sea. Mark suggested that we take a boat ride back to our hotel, being that it was such a pleasant afternoon. I wholeheartedly agreed, although admittedly, the last time I had been on a boat with Mark was on the Baltic Sea, when the Finnish police were chasing him across a casino ferry.

Mark and I bought tickets for our Thames River boat ride and found our seats, which were outside on the stern of the boat, on a bench that seemed to run around the edge. There were metal stanchions behind the bench that prevented people from falling backwards off the boat, but little else for protection. Mark placed his expensive bag of CDs between us, as we sat talking and enjoying the sunshine, which was a rare gift for a rock band on tour.

When the boat finally docked an hour later, we got up to make our way to the gangway, and that's when Mark realized that his bag of rare, folkloric CDs had disappeared. There was no way that it had been stolen because we had been sitting there the entire time, the bag between us. But somehow, one of us either bumped the bag, or perhaps it just slipped over the side, and we never noticed it fall into the river below.

Mark looked at me with a look that said, are you fucking kidding me, after all that? His rare CDs that had cost over 1,000 bucks were gone— just like our luck. I really had nothing to say, because a bag of rare CDs in the Thames seemed to be the perfect metaphor for everything we had been through as a band.

Somehow that bag of CDs, as unimportant as it might seem, represented something much bigger that had changed in music. The boy bands were just starting to get popular, the pop and hip hop groups were dominating radio, and songwriters like the Screaming Trees were becoming less and less relevant. We could all see it coming.

We still had a few more dates to play in England, so we soldiered on. Every night after the shows, and because I was sober, I would just go back to my hotel room and call it a night. There was no more partying for me, I was much more excited about eating a good meal, reading a book, and getting a good night's sleep. I was sound asleep when, at about 5 am, I got a call from Mark saying that he wanted to talk to me about something. He suggested that we go have an early breakfast because he was awake and quite hungry. This surprised me because Mark never seemed to eat very much, so I thought it was a good sign.

We met in the lobby and walked out into the chilly British morning, walking for a bit until we found a 24-hour bistro. We sat at a table near the back of the restaurant, and I distinctly remember that Mark ordered a Joe's Special, which is basically scrambled eggs mixed with ground beef and spinach, stir-fried together. I can't remember what I ordered, probably some kind of breakfast, but I was surprised by the way Mark wolfed down his Joe's Special, he seemed like the old healthy Mark. After we finished eating, he said he wanted to show me something.

He began to roll up his left sleeve, because with all the years that Mark had been doing heroin, his arms were perpetually covered in long sleeved shirts to hide the track marks that the needles caused. As he rolled his sleeve up and over his left elbow, I could see a huge, gaping hole in his arm, and in that hole, I could clearly see the white bone exposed inside the wound. It was a good thing he had waited to show me this until after we had finished eating our food.

"Jesus Christ Mark, what happened?" I said in disbelief. "It's an abscess that opened up," Mark replied. "What do you think, does it look bad?"

Apparently an abscess had developed in his arm where he had shot some heroin and it had finally opened up and ruptured, exposing layers of flesh and bone. It looked absolutely horrific, like a zombie's arm, made all the more ghoulish by the fact that it didn't bleed. I was actually in a bit of shock because it was not something I expected to see, and I couldn't believe that a person could be functional and speak in a relatively normal manner with a wound like that.

That's when I knew the Trees and all this touring had to end—as in, immediately. I said, in the most gentle but firm way that I could, "Mark, we have to stop touring right now, and I mean *right* now. We have to stop, and you've got to get medical help for this immediately. Your arm is going to get infected like it did in Montreal, you could get gangrene or blood poisoning and this time you could really lose your arm." That's basically what I said to him, although I probably stammered while speaking because I was pretty shaken. I do remember saying at the end, "This isn't what rock & roll is about, man. It's not worth dying for, and certainly not like this. We have to stop this madness and just go home, and you've got to get help."

Mark nodded in silent agreement because he knew, and then I added, "I'm going to talk to Peter and Cliff when our flight lands in New York."

I'd like to say that we went home the next day and stopped the insanity, but we didn't. We still played a few more shows in England, and then we finally headed home after that. I had our travel agent extend my time in New York City, so I could go see Peter and Cliff in person and talk about what was really happening to Mark and the band, out there on the dark road.

I sat down across from Peter in his Manhattan office (Cliff wasn't there this time) and I set the tone with a grave and detailed explanation about the hole in Mark's arm. "Peter, it is so much worse out there than you can imagine. Mark is going to die, either from an overdose or an infection if we keep this thing going. We have to stop, and I mean right now." I told him that we could always make money by touring, but Mark was just using that money to feed his habit and he would eventually die from it. I didn't want to be the drummer in the band when that happened, and I told Peter he could replace me or he could cancel all the remaining tour dates, right then. Regardless, we had to get Mark some help.

Peter paused for a few long seconds as he looked at me carefully, gauging the sincerity of my manner. This was unusual for him because he was famous for his rapid fire, machine gun responses. When he looked me directly in the eyes, I could see that he finally understood. "OK, I understand now and you're right. I'll cancel all of the Trees upcoming shows and we'll try to get Mark some help—if he'll take it."

With all historical accuracy and fairness, I think this was the moment when we saved Mark's life. We all loved him, despite his addiction and the unbelievable ordeals we had gone through with him—but we had to get him healthy.

What would happen next was entirely up to him.

A CRYPTIC PHONE CALL

Throughout 1997 the Trees were generally inactive, aside from a handful of shows that we played along the west coast. Those shows were entirely done so that we could all make some money. Mark was still not clean or sober, but he was better off than when we were on tour. He had fired Peter and Cliff for reasons that none of us understood, and we all prayed that he would eventually make the decision to go to rehab. In all honesty, I was waiting for the dreaded phone call that he had overdosed.

I kept myself busy and earned a little money by producing local bands in Seattle, and I did a US tour with Tuatara, my instrumental group that now had two albums out on Epic Records. Tuatara had also become a kind of go-to backing band for singer-songwriters, and we played shows with artists like Mark Eitzel, John Wesley Harding, and a few other singers that Peter Buck had brought into the fold.

By 1998, Mark had finally made the choice to go into rehab at an extended stay facility in the Los Angeles area. It had taken him the better part of a year to finally make the decision, but he was finally there. To give credit where it is definitely due, it was Courtney Love who paid for the whole thing, and it was an expensive check to write. I had stayed in touch with our old manager, Peter Mensch, and he's the one who told me that Courtney paid for it. People have said terrible things about Courtney over the years, but I will say that in the handful of times that I met her, she was always very polite and respectful to me. And when the chips were down, and Mark had nowhere else to go and no one else to help him, it was Courtney Love who stepped in to make sure Mark got the help he needed, so that his mind and body could truly heal.

The Trees were basically floating in an abyss of non-activity, and without the guidance of Peter and Cliff, we didn't know what we should even be doing as a band. Should we be writing songs, or should we start looking for new careers? I even thought about going back to the University of Washington to finish my abbreviated music degree. I think in our hearts we knew the band was over, and really we were just glad to have survived it all, Mark most especially.

Mark's arms had finally healed from the years of intravenous drugs, and when I saw him for the first time after his stay in rehab, he showed them to me. They looked like they had been put through a blast furnace, every inch completely scarred with discolored tissue, like a quilt of different colored skins. Mark joked that he and the Trees business manager had calculated that he had a shot a million dollars worth of heroin into his arms. I joked that he should call his solo band "Mark Lanegan & His Million Dollar Arms," and we both had a good laugh about that one.

Mark was trying to figure out what to do next with his life, where he should live, and all of the complexities that go with changing your life so completely. I was still living in my Craftsman bungalow on Phinney Ridge in Seattle, although my longtime girlfriend and I had finally broken up. I now had a roommate with Danny Baird, who was transitioning from being a tour manager, to being a regular manager for some young bands in Seattle. I lived upstairs on the top floor, Danny had the bedroom on the main floor, and I invited Mark to stay with us in the downstairs basement studio. It was a sober house, as Danny and I weren't drinking, and I figured Mark would be happy being around people who knew him and could help him stay on the path until he figured out where he wanted to go next.

Mark accepted my offer and moved into the basement studio, which had a sleeping area and its own entrance, and could have been a small apartment were it not filled with all my musical gear. The three of us got along quite well, considering our previously turbulent years on the road, but that's what sobriety usually brings—peace and stability.

I was also traveling a fair bit too, flying back and forth between Seattle and Los Angeles, where I had rented a small studio apartment in Hollywood. I was trying to keep my career going by playing drums and percussion on albums for other bands, picking up some production work on the side whenever I could. I ended up getting called in for recording sessions with bands like R.E.M., Stone Temple Pilots, and Josh Homme's new band, Queens Of The Stone Age. On these albums, I added drums, various exotic percussion, vibraphone, marimba, and even upright bass. I also recorded with some really talented but relatively unknown singer-songwriters, where I honed my skills as a producer. It was a good, positive time for me as I figured out a new path, a kind of slow and steady walk towards something musically different.

Danny was doing well too, he had started a house construction business like I used to do, and I even gave him most of my old tools to help him launch his new venture. He also helped Mark get his solo career back on track, which culminated in his third album, *Scraps At Midnight (1998)*. When we were all together at the house, we spent most of our time sitting on the back deck that I had built, chain smoking cigarettes, and looking westward at the beautiful Olympic Mountains and the magnificent sunsets that fell behind their peaks.

I have good memories of that time because we usually ate together on the back deck after I would fire up the barbecue, and we all laughed hysterically about the absolutely insane things that we had been through over the years. Jesus, what a time....

At one point, Mark and I even talked about doing a tour together with Tuatara serving as his backing band because he really liked the music that Peter Buck and I were experimenting with. We even had our booking agents explore the possibility of a tour, and there was serious interest from the promoters, but ultimately, Mark decided he just didn't want to go out on the road again, not for a long time.

I totally understood why, obviously.

I finally had a new girlfriend too, who was a model and business woman from Los Angeles. She was a lovely person, and although our relationship only lasted 6 months, it was a positive thing for both of us. She had flown up to spend the weekend with me at the Seattle house, and we planned on doing all the tourist stuff that one does when a guest comes to town. Danny was away visiting his girlfriend, but Mark was still at the house.

That evening, the phone rang on my landline—none of us had cell phones obviously, and I answered the phone. It was a strange voice that sounded African or Middle Eastern, and he asked to speak with Mark. I didn't ask who it was, but I went downstairs to tell Mark that he had a strange phone call. Mark came up and took the call, listened for a few seconds, and then suddenly hung up the phone, turning pale as he looked at me in disbelief. I asked him what the hell was going on and he simply replied, "The Somalis—they've found me."

I didn't ask for the details, but I knew from our past conversations on the back deck that Mark had had some bad dealings with these Somali drug dealers, who ruled a certain part of Seattle where Mark used to live. Somehow they had found out where he was staying and they had gotten my unlisted phone number, and this totally enraged me. As you can imagine from my experience touring with the Trees, being around the dingy circle of drug dealers and the drug fiends who followed them, made me despise every drug dealer we ever encountered. My hatred rose to the degree that I wanted them locked up in prison forever. Yet, here we were again, dealing with drug dealers, this time from Somalia, and they were harassing my friend in my own home, therefore they were harassing me as well. I might have been known as the nice, sober guy, but I also grew up on a farm in rural Washington where I was raised by real cowboys and loggers. My ire had been raised.

I told my now-concerned girlfriend what was going on, and that our weekend plans had to be modified. I was happy to fly her back to LA, first class, and pick up where we left off as soon as the drama had passed. Bad ass person that she was, she said she wanted to stay on anyway.

I went upstairs to my bedroom and grabbed the only weapon I owned (besides those Samurai swords from Philadelphia), which was my grandfather's 1950s Winchester 12 gauge shotgun, tucked away in the back of my closet. I had used it to shoot clay skeet when I was in high school, but I hadn't fired it in many years. I loaded it with shells, full to its limit, and went back downstairs.

I told Mark and my girlfriend very clearly, "If any one of those motherfuckers tries to come into this house, I will ventilate him on the spot." And I meant it.

That seemed to put Mark a little more at ease, but he was still shaken from the phone call. That night, Mark, my girlfriend, and I watched a movie in the living room just to change the mood, and then Mark eventually went back downstairs to the studio. It was quiet, dark, and safe down there.

I stayed up all night that first night, waiting for a knock at the door, or an attempted break-in. If they had my phone number they probably knew where I lived, but I'd be ready. At one point deep in the middle of the night, I noticed a sedan parked on the other side of our small street. This wasn't unusual in and of itself because cars parked there from time to time, however, being in the heightened state of awareness that I was, I was immediately suspicious. I opened the front door and walked out onto my porch, cradling the Winchester in my left elbow. I could see the glowing ember of a cigarette in the driver's seat, but I couldn't see a face, it was too dark. All of a sudden, however, the car started its engine and drove off down the street. Maybe it was the Somalis, or maybe it was just some innocent guy temporarily parked, who was shocked to see an armed man on a front porch. I'd drive away too if I saw that.

The next day and night were less tense, I slept upstairs with my girlfriend, but I kept the Winchester by the bed just in case. I think it was the third or fourth day after the cryptic phone call when Mark told me that as much as he appreciated my hospitality over the last few months, he really needed to get the hell out of Seattle permanently. That's when our mutual friend, the great Duff McKagan, opened his Los Angeles home to Mark, where he could stay for a much longer period of time. That's where Mark began the next phase of his life, and the resurrection of his solo career, down in sunny LA.

Mark never lived in Seattle again, although he did play several solo shows there in the following decades.

Technically, that little Craftsman bungalow, which I had bought and remodeled with Mad Season money, was the last official residence of Mark Lanegan in Seattle.

THE BUCK CONNECTION

Peter Buck's name pops up a lot in the saga of the Screaming Trees because he was a great supporter of the band, and he gave us some valuable advice at crucial points. Maybe it was because Peter, being the hugely successful songwriter and guitarist behind R.E.M., recognized a songwriting kinship with the Trees—or maybe he just loved our chaos. Whatever the case, Peter became one of my oldest friends from the early Seattle music scene, and his connection with the Trees bears some explanation.

I first met Peter in 1993, a couple years after he moved to Seattle to mix an R.E.M. album. He had also married a friend of mine, Stephanie Dorgan, the founder of the legendary *Crocodile Café*, which was the rock club at the epicenter of the Seattle music scene, our ground zero so to speak.

Upon Stephanie's recommendation, Peter invited me to come down to the Crocodile to play upright bass with a singer-songwriter he was working with named Kevin Kinney, who fronted the Atlanta rock band, Drivin N Cryin. His show at the Crocodile was a great success, we had a blast playing together, and I'm still friends with Kevin 30 years later, occasionally sitting in to play with him when he does a tour around the Pacific Northwest. In the three decades that followed, Peter Buck and I became great friends and we have worked on over 35 albums together, playing with other bands and singer-songwriters, including the beautiful song he wrote for Mad Season that Mark finished, "Black Book Of Fear."

During the same period of time that Mad Season was trying to make our second album, we found ourselves with three weeks of pre-paid studio time that was not going to be used. Thus, Mike McCready, Baker Saunders, and I decided to divide up that time into three blocks of one-week sessions, which each of us could use for our own projects. That's when I started the band Tuatara, with Peter Buck on guitar, saxophonist Skerik, and Justin Harwood from the band, Luna. In a strange, tangential way, Mad Season helped me get Tuatara started as well.

The initial success of Tuatara allowed us to do a full US tour with another singer that Peter and I had worked with, Mark Eitzel, formerly of the band, American Music Club. Almost every one of our shows on that tour was sold out, and some of them were in the same venues the Screaming Trees had previously played. Those experiences, along with Peter's encouragement, gave me the confidence to start thinking about a career as a producer/composer, rather than just being a drummer.

It was around the same period of time, in 1996, when Peter asked me to play percussion on the R.E.M. album already in progress, *New Adventures in Hi Fi (1996)*. It was being finished up in *Studio X* at *Bad Animals*, the same studio where we had mixed Mad Season. I showed up with my rather huge arsenal of percussion, much to the surprise and consternation of producer Scott Litt, who was absolutely not expecting me and a truckload of percussion. In fact, he actually seemed a little ticked off when I showed up at the studio, for reasons that I never understood—maybe Peter hadn't informed him that I was coming down? Still, I played percussion and vibraphone on several R.E.M. songs, and this led me to being invited to play on their next album, *UP*, which was recorded in Athens, GA, and San Francisco, CA during most of 1998. This was a massive opportunity for me as a musician, especially when R.E.M. invited me to join them as a touring member into the foreseeable future.

I had been a huge R.E.M. fan since the mid 1980s, when I first discovered their albums of highly original indie rock. They were songwriters through and through, and in fact, my first rock band in college back in 1985 played two R.E.M. songs in our live set, both of which I sang as I played drums. I also think it's fair to say that R.E.M. was a very big influence on the Seattle music scene, not necessarily in their musical style, but more so because of their artistic and financial success. This is because R.E.M. showed the Seattle bands, and presumably countless other bands around the world, that it was indeed possible to be an independent band that made albums of original music, and could also be financially successful with global touring over the course of decades. R.E.M. was really the first American rock band to do that, and half of their career was spent on an indie label.

It was in 1998 when I returned to Seattle after a long recording session with R.E.M in San Francisco. Mark Lanegan was now living at Duff McKagan's house in Los Angeles when he called to say, "Listen bro, we're talking about doing another Trees album if we can find a label to finance it. I don't have any real faith that this will happen, but if it does, we'd love to have you play drums. But I'll kill you if you quit R.E.M. to rejoin the Trees—you can't throw away an opportunity like that."

I think Mark knew that I had finally arrived at a good place, where I was now playing with a very big band that could harness my musical abilities much more than anything the Trees could offer. Yet there it was again, the distant possibility that the Trees could make another album. The voice in my head reminded me of how the Trees were still the best songwriting band in our peer group, and how could I not want to be part of that again? You have to do it, I thought to myself, because even with R.E.M. I was still a sideman playing their songs. With the Trees, I was the drummer and equal band member who got to co-write songs.

I didn't quit R.E.M. right away because I loved playing with them, but I kept it in my mind that another Trees album was a possibility, and I started writing songs in the event that it might actually happen.

It was early 1998 when the Trees finally reunited to work on another round of demos that we would use to try and get another record deal. Mark had found us a new manager, a kid really, named Brian Klein. Brian had been an understudy for the manager of Stone Temple Pilots, and Mark knew Scott Weiland, the singer of STP, so I presumed that's where the connection came from. Brian was young and smart, but he was not as experienced as the other managers we had worked with. However he was enthusiastic and wanted to represent the Trees, despite our tarnished reputation.

Simultaneous to all this, I completed my recording work for R.E.M.'s *UP* album, and I was rehearsing with them as their percussionist for a series of shows that would showcase their new songs. Unfortunately, R.E.M.'s original drummer, Bill Berry, had recently quit the band, and new drummers were being auditioned. Bizarrely, and even though I had actually played drums on some of R.E.M's new songs, I was not invited to audition for the drum spot. Instead, they wanted me to be the multi-instrumentalist who played all the other instruments, which I had played on their album. I was disappointed at first, but I agreed to continue as we rehearsed in Athens, GA. I played a variety of instruments on every song, while the drums were played by Joey Waronker, the former drummer of Beck, and the son of Lenny Waronker, the famed president of Warner Brothers Records.

As it turned out, I only played a handful of shows with R.E.M., the largest one being the massive Tibetan Freedom Concert at RFK stadium in Washington, D.C. During the first day of the two-day festival, a lightning bolt struck the stadium, injuring some of the fans, which caused the first day to be cut short, and that meant the R.E.M. show would have to be rescheduled for the following day. This led to a subsequent riot in the stadium, and the bands were hurriedly taken to various bunkers under the stadium until the chaos subsided. I found myself in a tiny cramped room lit by a single light bulb where, to my left, were members of various bands, and exactly to my right shoulder was Brad Pitt and his partner at the time, Jennifer Aniston. Everyone was calm and cool headed, and we made jokes in the dim darkness. These are the bizarre situations and the interesting people you meet when you play rock & roll at that level.

When the "all clear" was given to leave the bunkers, the bands began to disperse, only to find that there was still a melee in progress. That's when a chaotic, mad dash to the tour buses began, with band members and their crews running in circles, confused as to where they should go. I thought it would be an easy walk back to the bus, but as it turned out, the R.E.M. bus had already left without me. What happened to the no man left behind policy? I waved down a random bus, and fortunately they were gracious enough to take me back to my hotel.

I have to say, the riot itself didn't bother me that much—that's just rock & roll, and you have to expect that kind of thing from time to time. Being held in a bunker with movie stars didn't bother me either, again, it's just part of the job. But the fact that I was left behind by a band I was playing with left me a little concerned. The Trees would have never left me behind, in fact, the Trees would have stayed and singlehandedly fist-fought the entire mob, side-by-side, arms raised against any and all who dared to attack the mighty Screaming Trees.

The R.E.M. show was held the following day, and we played a good, if rather subdued set, largely because most of the songs we played had not been released yet, and that confused the audience a bit. But it was when we played R.E.M.'s biggest hit that I realized where my place was. We started playing "Losing My Religion," and my instrument for that song was a synthesizer that played samples of the string arrangement. There I was, the former linebacker/drummer of the Screaming Trees, as infamous for brawling as drumming (which are not so philosophically different) and I was playing a synthesizer sample with my single, right index finger, standing perfectly still. It was just wrong, and not where I was supposed to be.

It was a couple weeks later when I gave notice to R.E.M. that I would be leaving the band. I wrote an incredibly well-composed resignation letter, which Michael Stipe told me was one of the best letters he had ever received. "You know Barrett, we've fired people before, but you're the first guy to actually quit," he said with a laugh. I replied, "I know, and I love R.E.M., but my heart just isn't in it the way it should be. It's better that I leave now, before I get fired down the road."

I'm still friends with the R.E.M. guys, in fact in 2022, I played a couple of R.E.M tribute shows where some of the band members actually got on stage to play several of their songs—and I got to play drums. I still love their songs because they were exceptional songwriters, and they made some of the greatest rock albums of the 1980s and 1990s. I just couldn't be who I was a musician if I had stayed in that situation, and that's just the hard truth about music. Sometimes you have to make a very hard decision, and you absolutely must follow what your soul tells you to do. For me, my soul told me to stay with the Screaming Trees and see it through to the very end.

Admittedly, Peter was pretty mad at me for a time because after all, it was he who got me the job in R.E.M. in the first place. We eventually put it all behind us because real friends move beyond those kinds of things, and they become tiny hiccups in the scope of the larger work that Peter and I have done together.

Back in Screaming Trees world, several things were in the works, and the first phone call I made was to Peter to tell him that the Trees were going to make another album. "Would you be interested in playing some guitar on it?" I asked, somewhat hesitantly that he might rebuff me.

"Oh, hell yes!" Peter replied.

Because as Spike Lee once said, "Game recognizes game."

A FINAL BOW

All four of the Trees were back in Seattle now, Mark was temporarily staying at a hotel, and Lee presented us with a series of demos that were very good, exceptional even. They still needed tweaking and arranging, but the overall quality was great. They would also need to be recorded properly if we were going to present them to a label, so we started making a plan on how to accomplish this.

Our attorney had gotten the band released from our very exploitive contract with Epic Records, which the band had called home for nearly a decade. We had never been paid any royalties beyond our publishing because the band had a royalty rate of about 10%, which meant that all the money we had spent making albums and videos had to be recouped against our measly 10%, while Sony kept the other 90% as profit. This was not an uncommon record deal back then, but this is also why major label bands rarely get ahead and make any real money, when they are always indebted to a label that finds every possible way to not pay them.

The Trees devised a strategy to record an entire album of new material, and then see if we could find a new label where we could start with zero debt and possibly, just maybe, make a little money. The immediate problem was that the band had no money in its bank account to even record the songs—but I did. The Mad Season and Tuatara royalties had finally started to come in, and I had made more money on those albums than I had made with the Trees in the previous decade. I volunteered to pay for the recording sessions under the premise that I'd get paid back as soon as we got a record deal.

We ran the sessions in three blocks, the first of which was held at Stone Gossard's *Studio Litho*, in the Fremont neighborhood of Seattle. Stone is of course Pearl Jam's founding guitarist, and he gave me a great deal on the studio rate because he too loved the Trees, and this allowed us take our time and record the songs properly. I was the defacto producer of the sessions, simply because I was the most organized with our time, but the band didn't need a whole lot of poking and prodding—we had been doing this for years. The songs sounded fantastic, and we arranged them on the spot as we recorded them. We also had Peter Buck playing with us on his trademark Rickenbacker electric 12-string, which added extra luster to the tracks. The sessions went off without a hitch, we all got along great, and I think the sobriety element in the band was the main common denominator that kept us all focused and on the same goal.

The second session was held at Martin Feveyear's studio in a different part of Seattle, near the entrance of Discovery Park. Martin, if you'll remember, was the British sound engineer we hired on that first European tour in 1992 to drive our milk truck/equipment van. He had worked his way up the Trees ladder to become our monitor engineer, then our front of house engineer, and now Martin was living in Seattle working out of his own recording studio, *Jupiter Studios*. It was a small but effective space where we recorded some additional songs, and then we rough mixed everything that we had recorded between the two studios. It was now ready to present to some record labels.

Our new manager, Brian Klein, thought we should try a third session with the big name producer, Toby Wright. Toby had produced several hugely successful albums in the past, including the classic Alice In Chains album, *Dirt (1992)*, which we all loved. We thought we'd give Toby a try and see if something new and different might emerge.

Down to Los Angeles we went, but this time we were only able to track two more songs, one being the song, "Crawl Space," and the other being an alternate version of "Anita Grey," which we had previously recorded at *Studio Litho*.

The sessions with Toby went OK, but it was not as fluid as it had been when it was just the band and Peter Buck, recording in our hometown. Having a producer who we really didn't know that well sort of hampered our progress rather than accelerating it. Additionally, we had brought back our rhythm guitarist, Josh Homme, to play on these last couple of songs because he had given the Trees an excellent sound when he toured with us for the *Dust* album. Josh had moved back to Los Angeles and was preparing to record his second album with Queens Of The Stone Age, *Rated R (2000),* which is the album I played on, where I added percussion, vibraphone, and steel drums.

Mark would also sing on that superb album, and in fact, Van Conner and I had played as a rhythm section on some of Josh's early demos at the *Rancho de la Luna* studio in Joshua Tree, CA. We all knew how good Josh's new band was shaping up to be, and that's also why we wanted him in the studio with us for that last Trees session.

Since the *Dust* tour and the formation of Queens Of The Stone Age, Josh had developed some very strong opinions about music and his own production ideas, which often clashed with Toby Wright's ideas. I think Josh's ideas were valid, but Toby wanted to change the arrangements and the style of our music, and this approach didn't work that well. Thus, the sessions got a little tense towards the end, and we ended up only recording those two songs.

We were done with recording and wanted to present the rough mixes of the album to some labels, so with a dozen really good, well-recorded songs, we set up a showcase on September 12th, 1998 at the *Roxy Theatre* in Hollywood, right on the Sunset Strip. The show was sold out, but more importantly there were A&R reps from every label in Los Angeles. The Trees were such a good live band, who wouldn't want to see that spectacle? We all thought a record deal would be imminent, perhaps even a bidding war would ensue between the labels. Unfortunately the opposite happened, and not a single offer came in from any of the labels.

I think, because of our pre-existing reputation as unpredictable hell-raisers, and our track record of lower than expected album sales, the Trees were just too much of a financial risk. The labels all wanted to see us play live, that's what we were known for, and I think they truly loved the band. But putting their money behind us was a different matter. That was it for the Trees, we thought. We went from a whisper to a scream, and back to a whisper with that Los Angeles showcase.

We did play a couple other Hollywood shows in February of 2000, and these were held at Johnny Depp's club, *The Viper Room,* also on the Sunset Strip. Again, no labels were interested, and that's when the band finally decided to throw in the towel. We did, however, get asked to play one final show on June 25th, 2000, at Seattle's Memorial Stadium. This was to commemorate the opening of what was at the time called the Experience Music Project, a music museum designed by architect Frank Gehry to house the enormous music collection of Microsoft co-founder, Paul Allen. The event paid us about ten times more money than any show we had ever done before, so it was a good final payday for the band. Since it was our last, bowing out performance, we also invited Peter Buck and Josh Homme to join us for this last hurrah—why not have all six of us on stage at the same time? It was actually a really fantastic show, and that can't always be said about bands that know they are breaking up. Often a band's final show ends in a brawl, and that could have very easily been the case with the Trees.

Instead, we went out on that stage as friends, in our hometown of Seattle.

LAST WORDS

It's funny how the passage of time can change your perspective on things because when the Trees played that final show in June of 2000, we left the stage thinking that that was the end of it.

But eleven years later, in 2011, I was talking to Mark about an unrelated music project I was working on, and we started talking about the recordings we had made in 1998 when the Trees were looking for a record deal. I had found the original rough mixes on a CD in one of my boxes, along with the two songs that Toby Wright had recorded in LA. I sent the mixes to Mark, and he agreed that they were still really great songs, regardless of the time that had elapsed since we recorded them—a great song is a great song, no matter when it was written. We agreed that they should be released as some kind of album, and since I had my own imprint label with Sony Distribution, the band agreed that I should release the album so that the band could own the copyright and control the ownership.

The only thing Mark wanted to make clear to the public was that these were the band's final recordings, and not an attempt at a new album. We needed to somehow advertise this fact in the album title so I came up with, *Last Words: The Final Recordings,* which was taken from one of the songs Lee had written, "Last Words."

At this point, I contacted Jack Endino to do the final mixes, since Jack had worked with the Trees numerous times, including several B-Sides that we had done with him for Epic Records.

I retrieved the magnetic tapes from Martin Feveyear's *Jupiter Studio,* where they had been stored for over a decade in a closet. Jack then began the process of "baking the tapes," which is a technique whereby old magnetic tapes are baked in an oven to warm up the tape surface, and make it more pliable for the transfer from analog tape to digital hard drive. In Jack's method, his version of baking a tape involved an old fruit drying machine from the 1970s, which was round and exactly the same size and shape of a 2" reel of magnetic tape. If you knew Jack personally the way we did, the fact that he discovered a fruit dryer to perfect this technique makes perfect sense.

Once we had the songs transferred into the digital realm, Jack and I started editing and mixing the songs. I added or replaced a few minor overdubs on a handful of songs, playing vibraphone, shaker, and tambourine, but the original recordings were still in pristine condition and we left them untouched. Mark's vocals were astoundingly good because he was finally sober when he sang those vocal tracks. Van and Lee also played incredibly well, and having the guest guitarists of Peter and Josh made it all sound very glued together. Perhaps most importantly, the songs themselves still held up as great examples of the Trees songwriting ability, which is the reason why Mark and I thought the album should be released to the public.

When it came time to sequence and master the album, I called my long time mastering engineer, Chris Hanzsek, who helped finalize the album for CD, LP, and digital formats. The band agreed on using all of the songs I had produced from the *Studio Litho* and *Jupiter* sessions, but we only used one song from the Toby Wright sessions. That gave us 10 great songs for the album.

Now it was time to put the artwork together, and this is when Mark started sending me the most absurdly hilarious album covers I have ever seen. Mark was fully enmeshed in his solo career, having made numerous albums and some incredibly good collaborations with Queens Of The Stone Age and Isobel Campbell. This had caused Mark to join the digital revolution and buy a computer, and that's how his artwork images started coming to me through the wires. They included things like two rhinoceroses humping in a swamp; an extremely obese ballerina in a yellow tutu; a freight train derailed with wreckage all around. These were just some of the images that Mark sent me for the *Last Words* cover art, usually with a tag line that said something like, "I think this sums up our band," or "This image really captures the moment."

It was true, Mark's images actually captured the huge, brutal, often destructive power of the Screaming Trees, but we sure as hell couldn't put that on an album cover.

I would email Mark back with whatever witty comment I could muster, but right then another absurd photo would come through, more hilarious and insane than the previous. I was laughing constantly on my end, because Mark really did have the most wicked sense of humor.

Ultimately, and in a much more elegant mindset, we decided on a piece of art by a young artist named Erin Currier, who I had met many years earlier when I lived in Taos, New Mexico in the early 2000s. Erin is now a globally famous artist, but in 2011, she was more well known in New Mexico than anywhere else. Erin's painting, which the Trees universally loved, was of a Latin American restaurant worker holding a silver platter with a pistol on top. This gun-toting man was based on the true story of a waiter who helped assassination a corrupt Latin American dictator. The image worked perfectly for our album, especially with the title, *Last Words*.

When we finally released the album on August 2nd, 2011, many of our fans were elated and thought the band might reunite to play shows again. We didn't, of course, and by this time in music history, digital downloading had replaced physical products by a huge margin, so the album eventually settled into the streaming universe, where it still exists today.

The critics seemed to be split on the album—some loved it, others didn't, but who trusts a music critic anyway? However, they all generally agreed:

The Screaming Trees were always about the songwriting, first and foremost.

INSPIRATION IS FOR AMATEURS

In the ensuing years after the Trees formally disbanded, numerous opportunities were presented to each of us, but other things had to be taken care of. Because when a band officially breaks up, especially when it's a relatively big band that has been doing business for many years, there are legal and financial matters that have to be attended to. Things like, the sunset accounting, which is when the business manager wraps up all the loose ends and closes down various business entities that have existed for different purposes. Touring companies are dissolved, record labels and publishing companies are informed of the band's decision to disband, and various legal affairs are decided upon as the whole carnival packs up and leaves town.

With the Trees, each of us had already started to make inroads with other projects, sometimes even starting new bands. None of us waited around for someone else to make something magical happen, we just kept doing what we always did, but now on separate paths. As the artist Chuck Close once said, "Inspiration is for amateurs," meaning that you don't just sit on your ass waiting for the lightning bolt to strike. A professional artist goes inward and finds the inspiration in the praxis of their craft, it's in the *doing* of the art itself because in the doing comes the very inspiration needed to create something new. All of the greatest artists in every tradition have figured out this noble truth, usually the hard way, which is the same way we all did.

Van had already married his wife Jill when the band was still active, and they decided to start a family and have children, which made Van a father of three. He had to support his growing family, so he got a steady job with a Washington utility company, but that didn't stop him from starting a new rock band called, Valis, which was named after a Philip K. Dick novel. This new band featured a different Conner brother, the younger Patrick, who was the same kid who used to house sit for us at the Green Lake house when we were on tour in the early 1990s. Valis went on to make 5 studio albums, and they did the occasional tour of the US and Europe.

Having a family and a regular job meant that Van had to make his musical life based in Washington, so he kept his feet in that world by starting a recording studio in the Fremont neighborhood of Seattle. He called his new studio, *Strange Earth,* where many bands have recorded and still do to this day, including myself. I've recorded and filmed several projects there, and *Strange Earth* was also the last studio where Soundgarden rehearsed and recorded before the death of Chris Cornell. It's an important place, a sacred space, both historically and musically, especially now that Van has passed on as well.

Gary Lee, on his new path, literally followed the noble truth of the artist by continuing to write songs, just as he always had. He also married when the Trees were still active, to his longtime girlfriend, Dr. Janet, a chemistry professor at a small Texas college. They also had a daughter, and Lee found his happiness as a stay at home dad who raised their daughter, wrote more songs, and released 5 excellent solo albums.

Mark had the most prominent and successful post-Trees career, as he continued to make groundbreaking solo albums, and tour the world with a band he had assembled in Belgium of all places. He told me he did this because Europe was always the most receptive place for his music so it made sense to have a band based over there, rather than a bunch of Americans that he would have to fly over every time he wanted to do a tour. Mark also continued his ongoing collaboration with Queens Of The Stone Age, where he sang and co-wrote songs, most famously on their breakthrough hit album, *Songs For The Deaf (2002).*

The records Mark made with Isobel Campbell were also, in my opinion, some of the most beautiful singing that Mark ever did in his long and storied career. I think he realized that his incredible voice worked well in many different settings—with Queens Of The Stone Age, with Isobel, and in other songwriting partnerships with people like Alain Johannes, Greg Dulli, and Duke Garwood. I don't know how many people Mark collaborated with, it seemed like there were many, and most seemed to be one-off experiments, but it appears that he loved the spirit of collaboration as much as making his own records.

For myself, I decided to take an entirely different approach. I wasn't interested in getting married or having children because the truth is, many people like me choose to explore the world and continue to learn about it, without the responsibility of raising a family. Instead, I chose a path that combined both academic and artistic disciplines, which took me to some incredible places.

There were twists and turns that I could never have imagined.

A ROAD LESS TRAVELED

For my own journey, one of the things I was determined to do was travel. Not in a rock band on a tour bus, but actual on the ground, deep in the rainforest kind of travel. During the last few years of the Trees, I had been splitting time between my house in Seattle and the apartment I had rented in Hollywood, where I was getting a lot of experience in the recording studios of Los Angeles. I was learning how to be a session drummer, as well as a producer, and I even worked on some film soundtracks. The very first soundtrack I composed was for a film called *Lush (2000)*, and it helped get the film into the Sundance Film Festival, which was a huge achievement.

It was album production, however, that came most naturally to me, in that I found that I was very good at being in the studio with a band and helping them to realize a unified, sonic vision. I could focus on the musician's abilities to bring out their best performances, both individually and as a group. And especially where songwriting was concerned, I had so much experience shredding tunes with the Screaming Trees, Mad Season, Tuatara, and even peripherally working with R.E.M., the songwriting aspect became the primary focus in my work as a producer. Because if you were a Screaming Tree, you knew that the craft of songwriting had to be the top priority, otherwise why are you even recording? You might be an entertainer of some sort and that's fine too, the world will always need a court jester. But if you want to change the hearts and minds of people, then songwriting and album production becomes a very different career path from all the other art forms. That's why we call it, *The Invisible Art.*

The other thing that seized me in the final years of the Screaming Trees was the importance of world music. I know that might sound strange to people who think that rock musicians only listen to rock music, however if you look at some of the most innovative musicians in history, rock or otherwise, you will often find a common thread where they were either influenced by world music, or they directly collaborated with world musicians.

The Beatles went to India to learn from Ravi Shankar; Led Zeppelin went to Morocco to absorb the Arabic melodies; The Rolling Stones' Brian Jones had an obsession with the Jajouka musicians; the saxophonist Wayne Shorter went to Brazil to collaborate with the singer Milton Nascimento; the drummer Ginger Baker went to Nigeria to play with Fela Kuti; the songwriter Paul Simon went to South Africa to work with Ladysmith Black Mambazo; guitarist Ry Cooder made multiple trips to Cuba, and this culminated with his incredible production of *Buena Vista Social Club (1997)*.

The list goes on and on of the greatest musicians in history and their interest in global music, so I too went looking for more musical inspiration. As a drummer, first and foremost, I felt a spiritual pull to explore the exotic rhythms of the world, because for me, the Seattle music scene had become littered with dead friends and former band mates. I needed to find inspiration out in the greater world, and I needed to study the ABCs of drumming, which in drumming lore is Africa, Brazil, and Cuba. Magically, I got to visit all three.

In 1997, I made the first of several solo trips, this time to Central America, where I flew to Belize under the initial plan of visiting a cousin on her farm. The trip evolved into an unexpected drumming adventure, where I met and played with the legendary Garifuna drummers of Hopkins Village.

Then in 1998, I had an opportunity to study with a Senegalese Wolof drum master, a *Griot*, as his tradition called him. This was a man I had studied with in Seattle, but he also took students back to Dakar, Senegal, where they could study directly with members of his family, which were some of the greatest drummers in Senegal. My trip included some additional study in Ghana, a country east of Senegal, where I took drumming classes at the University of Legon. This is where I learned a sacred truth that changed my understanding of drumming forever because in Ghana, they say that rhythm is the Earth, and singing is the Spirit, and both need the other to express themselves. This explained perfectly my relationship with Mark, Layne, and every singer I ever worked with, and why such a powerful dynamic existed between us.

Then in 1999, I was asked to participate in a music diplomacy program called, *The Music Bridge*, which sent musicians from the United States to different countries around the world to build musical bridges between their respective countries. In my case, I was invited to Havana, Cuba, along with about 100 other artists, some of them quite famous. Musicians like Bonnie Raitt, Mick Fleetwood, Michael Franti, Stewart Copeland, Andy Summers, and Burt Bacharach were just some of the musicians involved in the project. When I mentioned the program to my old friend Peter Buck, he asked if I could get him on the trip, which of course I did, and we had an incredible adventure in Cuba. I'll say this for the record too: the best musicians I have ever encountered anywhere in the world are the Cubans. They just absolutely outplay everyone, so if you go there, prepare to be humbled.

We ended up spending two hugely creative weeks in Havana based out of the Hotel Nacional, where we wrote songs and recorded with some of the top musicians in Cuba. To finish off this incredible experience, we were invited to play a concert at the old Charlie Chaplin Theater, followed by an invite to the presidential palace. There, we met then-president, Fidel Castro, in a diplomatic receiving line, one of the most surreal experiences of my life.

I'm certainly not a communist, nor do I support fascist dictators of any kind, foreign or domestic. Neither am I one who believes that capitalism will save our world from the problems we currently face, indeed, most of our problems have been created by both capitalism and communism combined. But I learned a lot just from observing how elegantly the Cubans lived their lives under extreme hardship, and the way they showed their beautiful humanity. I don't have a solution to the economic problems of the world, but being a world-traveling musician has helped me to see much more about how the people of the world survive with their regional difficulties. It has also shown me how important music is to the world, and to its people.

By the time the new century and the year 2000 rolled around, I found myself working with another global musician, the Brazilian singer and songwriter, Nando Reis. It was my old friend, Jack Endino, who called me in to play drums on Nando's new album, which he was producing in Seattle, and that's how I found myself playing Nando's highly popular form of Brazilian rock & roll. Nando invited me to tour Brazil when the album came out, so by the end of 2000, I had an apartment in the Ipanema neighborhood of Rio de Janeiro, and I was playing shows all over Brazil. It was my first time being in a band after the break up of the Screaming Trees, and it was an absolutely incredible experience to be touring in a huge musical country like Brazil.

At this point, I have played on almost all of Nando's many albums, and I also produced his first Latin Grammy-winning album, *Jardim-Pomar* (2017). In fact, portions of this book were written while I was living in Sao Paulo producing another of Nando's albums, Uma *Estrela Misteriosa (2024)*.

With this 20 plus year adventure I have had with Brazilian music, with Africa and Cuba before that, I had finally completed my ABCs of drumming. This is also why I have realized that, as much as I've learned about rhythms around the world, I still know very little. Because to become a master requires a life long quest of ever-increasing knowledge.

The 7 years between 1997 and 2003 were incredible, magical, evolutionary years for me. I was not attached to anyone or anything, and I really just explored the world and all of the music I could do within it. Between all the various adventures I undertook in those years, perhaps the single most important event that changed the course of my life was the time I spent studying with a Zen Master at the Detroit Street Zen Center in Hollywood.

During those years in the late 1990s and early 2000s, I lived in an apartment that had a Zendo on its ground floor, and there I could meditate in the evenings after my studio sessions had ended. This practice of Zen meditation also included the study of ancient manuscripts, as well as a life philosophy that I practice to this day. And that is how, after years of relapses and slip ups, I finally attained complete and total sobriety. In learning how to sit, meditate, and slow the movement of my chattering, monkey-mind, I saw that my true path was not to be a drunk, depressed, semi-successful musician. I saw that I could truly awaken myself, which is an ongoing process, to become the person I really wanted to be. Someone who deeply understood the connection between music and spirit, and who could channel that knowledge into everything I did.

Because to paint with sound is the ultimate spiritual practice.

SHAMANIC ADVENTURES

By 2003, and after returning from my second tour of Brazil with Nando Reis, I was now living full time in New Mexico. This is a state I had driven through multiple times in the middle of the night while on tour, perhaps stopping in Albuquerque for gas on the way from Texas to Arizona. Now I was living there, in the small, historic, wild west town of Taos.

I had gone there initially because my girlfriend at the time had introduced me to a group of martial artists, painters, and writers who really captured my attention. I decided that I had to live amongst them and learn their artistic philosophies, which were very inspiring. I was happy to stay in Taos until I figured out where I was going to go next on this unfolding, unpredictable adventure I had undertaken.

I became good friends with many of those artists, but as it turned out, what New Mexico really had to offer me was a chance to return to college and finish the music degree I had started in the mid 1980s, but stopped when rock & roll took over my life. I enrolled as an undergraduate at the University of New Mexico, where over the course of the next five years, I finished a bachelor's degree and a master's degree in anthropology, with a focus in ethnomusicology and linguistics.

Ethnomusicology is the academic study of world music, something I had already been doing "in the field" with my numerous music projects around the world. At the university, however, I learned much more about theoretical ideas and field methods at a level I couldn't have comprehended until I was sober and ready to be a student again.

In the summer of 2004, as I was preparing to start graduate school, I was offered the incredibly rare opportunity to do field work with an indigenous tribe in the Peruvian Amazon Rainforest. This project would have me working directly with the Shipibo Shamans, the Shipibo being the largest indigenous group in the Upper Peruvian Amazon. These shamans are renowned for their singing and healing abilities, which use sacred songs called *icaros* as the main healing modality.

Singing and healing are synonymous practices for the Shipibo, so my academic assignment would be to record as many of their healing *icaros* as possible, and then document their ceremonies. After that part was completed, I would then work directly with the Shipibo to create an album of their music, the royalties of which would go directly to the shamans and their families.

It was a perfect assignment, using all of the skills I had been developing over the years. I got to use my academic training, as well as my experience as an engineer and album producer. It was also a huge technical undertaking, especially in a place as wild as the Amazon Rainforest, but I was ready for it, this was my next musical adventure.

The entire experience literally changed my life forever because it taught me that music is not just limited to guitar chords, or drum rhythms, or even the human voice. Music in the Amazon Rainforest is literally emanating from every cell in every living thing that's alive down there—the rainforest itself, the shamans, the animals, the birds, the insects, and even the wind and the rain. The shamans also helped me to find my own singing voice again, which had been neglected after I stopped singing backing vocals in the Screaming Trees. In the Amazon Rainforest, I was surrounded by ancient trees that literally screamed music, 24 hours a day.

Suddenly I was singing to myself in the rainforest, composing new music with vocal melodies that were magically coming into my consciousness, out of thin air. It was previously impossible for me to do this kind of composing, where my voice became the writing instrument because I always had to sit down at a piano or play my upright bass to write music. Now I had music in my head, all the time, and it was even in my dreams, as I slept in my hammock in my thatched roof hut.

I had been doing Ayahuasca ceremonies with the shamans too, which is a powerful psychedelic, and this process had obviously opened up my musical perceptions. Their eldest and most revered shaman,

Enrique Sinuiri, confirmed this when he said, "Marteen, now you have drunk from the rainforest's medicine and she is inside of you, forever. Wherever you go in the world, no matter where you are, the rainforest will always be with you."

There was something incredibly beautiful and infinitely powerful about these shamans, and they helped me to see how the actual Universe was inside my mind, and that there was no separation between me, the rainforest, the birds, the plants, the people, or my life in music. It was all *the same thing*, and it was beautiful.

The Western, American, Judeo-Christian culture that I had been born into had totally evaporated. There was no god above me, and certainly no devil below. In fact, I saw that everything was sacred, and there was no hierarchy aside for the mutual respect of life. Everything else was just an imprinted idea, a series of invented stories, most of which had been made up by European patriarchs in the 4th century.

Here in the rainforest, the shamans revealed these truths, and it was exactly the same thing that the ancient Zen masters had been saying for thousands of years: It's all one interconnected thing, a tapestry of consciousness, and I am just a tiny manifestation of that infinity.

That experience was literally 20 years ago as of the writing of this book, and in that time, the Shipibo Shamans have become world famous for their medicine, and particularly for their transcendent singing. The three albums I have produced for the Shipibo over the last 20 years have earned them many thousands of dollars, and it has helped to raise attention about the sacred importance of the Amazon Rainforest. And here's a big secret that very few people have come to realize: It isn't the Ayahuasca medicine that causes the healing, although that is certainly part of the process. It's really the singing of the sacred *icaros*, which does the real healing.

When I came back from Peru in 2004, I finished writing my thesis, I turned in the field recordings I had made, and I produced that first album for the Shipibo Shamans titled, *Woven Songs Of The Amazon* (2006). It brought the Shipibo Shamans global fame.

I also recorded my first solo album, *The Painted Desert* (2004), which was something I'd started but hadn't been able to finish until I worked with the Shipibo. That trip to the rainforest unlocked something inside of me, and suddenly I could hear music in a completely different way. The melodies kept coming long after I returned from the rainforest, and 10 solo albums later, I'm still going.

After finishing my master's degree, I decided that I had had enough of the New Mexican desert and I moved back to Seattle—I had been gone for almost 10 years. I wasn't in a band and I didn't want to join one—I still had strong memories about Seattle in the 1990s. Instead, I applied for a job as a music professor at the small liberal arts college, Antioch University, where I joined the faculty as an adjunct professor of music. I designed several classes for the university, which were built around the study of music as an expression of culture, and my classes were almost always full.

Although I discovered that I had a great love for teaching, especially with college students who were there because they wanted to be there, I found that producing albums was still my greatest love. So after 7 years of teaching at Antioch, I decided that producing albums would be a far more expansive way of reaching people, than 20 or 30 students in a classroom.

In 2017, the year that I left teaching, I won my first Latin Grammy for producing another album for my Brazilian friend, Nando Reis. That same year, I published my first book about music around the world, *The Singing Earth (2017),* and the success of that book reminded me that good storytelling is also part of who I am. You're currently holding my 4th book (or listening to the audio book), so I have clearly committed myself to the cause.

That epic decade of the 1990s with the Screaming Trees had led me around the world and onto an entirely new path that I could have never imagined. From hard rock and alcoholism, to sobriety and academia, to producing albums around the world, my life became something much more enjoyable than the so-called pinnacle of rock stardom. And for that musical experience with the Screaming Trees, I am eternally grateful to Mark Lanegan, Gary Lee Conner, and Van Conner.

They welcomed me into their shamanic brotherhood and started me on the journey of a lifetime.

REUNION

In the 23 years since the Screaming Trees played our final show, and despite whatever the books and media might have said, the truth is that the four of us became friends again. The fact that we ended the band amicably, playing our final show with unity and pride is in and of itself a testament to that evolution. We all supported each other's later work, especially Mark with his solo career. He continued to play shows that incorporated classic Trees songs into his live show, and the collective feeling amongst the band was, we did good, but our time was up.

In the summer of 2012, I started jamming with Duff McKagan and Mike McCready again. A little known fact is that Duff and Mike had grown up in the same Seattle neighborhood, and had both attended Roosevelt High School together. Mike and I of course had our Mad Season history, but in the late 1990s when I lived in Los Angeles, Duff and I had tried to form a band with Sen Dog of Cypress Hill. We wrote songs and made a pretty cool demo, but nothing ever came of it.

Fast forward to 15 years later, and Duff, Mike, and myself started writing and recording songs at Mike's home studio, in the hopes that we might find "the singer" so that we could start a new band. After writing several instrumental tunes that were left wide open for vocals, Duff and Mike decided that they wanted to ask Mark Lanegan to join our band.

I was surprised by their choice, only because the list of potential singers we could have approached was pretty impressive. "Look," I said, "I really love Mark, he's a brother, and he's probably the greatest singer of our generation. But he was in the Trees for 15 years, and then he did Queens Of The Stone Age after that. I'm pretty sure he doesn't want to do the rock thing anymore, I think he's just focused on doing his solo albums."

Duff and Mike still wanted to try and persuade Mark, so they flew to Los Angeles to have lunch with him and present the new songs we had sketched out. I wasn't surprised when a couple days later, Duff told me that Mark had passed on our project. I knew that he would, only because I knew that Mark was an artist who had a vision for what he wanted to do, and joining another rock band just wasn't part of the equation.

Then in the summer of 2015, just four years after the release of the Screaming Trees' *Last Words* album, and the same year that Mad Season had reunited to play with Chris Cornell, Mark called me to tell me something I never expected. Apparently the Screaming Trees had been sent an offer by a promoter who wanted us to play a festival, and the performance fee was $100,000 for a one hour set. It was twice as much as we were paid for our final show in 2000, and it was about 10 times more than the average guarantee we used to get when we played theaters in the 1990s.

Mark and I talked on the phone about the possibility of doing the show, but we ultimately decided that it was too short a notice to do it that year. He and I were the only two members of the Trees who were still actively touring and playing music live, so it would have taken a lot of work to get the Trees firing on all cylinders again. Perhaps we could do the festival the following year, which would be a better time for us anyway, and maybe we could add a few more festivals around the same period of time and make it a financially respectable mini-tour.

This is the main point I want to re-emphasize about how the Trees were on good terms, we were talking to each other, and we were actually considering a reunion tour for 2016. It made perfect sense too, because Mark was playing Trees songs throughout his solo career, and he loved those final recordings we had done together. Here was our chance to do a victory lap, make a whole bunch of money, and maybe even have some fun rather than a grueling tour where we're still trying to "make it."

Throughout the remainder of 2015 and into 2016, Mark and our booking agents—the late Steve Strange (Mark's agent), and Steve Zapp (my agent) worked together as a team to look at show possibilities for the proposed Screaming Trees reunion tour. These shows largely focused on Europe and the UK, with a few high profile American festivals as well. As I've said before, the Trees were always much bigger in Europe,

Australia, and South America than they ever were in the United States, largely because those are continents where a great rock band can still draw a large audience, even today. Mark's solo career was evidence of this, and I did more album production work outside the United States than in it.

We communicated with our agents regularly as they started putting the numbers together, and Mark and I spoke on the phone often during this period of time. We both agreed that we'd need a fifth member to play rhythm guitar, but Josh Homme wasn't an option anymore because of his success with Queens Of The Stone Age. "What about Peter Buck?" I suggested, "He's played with us before and he loves us." "Give him a shout and see what he says," Mark replied. I called Peter immediately right after the call, and Peter's first words were, "Hell Yes!" Peter knew that playing in the Screaming Trees was always going to be a rocket ride, and you couldn't say no to that.

When the financial figures came back from our booking agents, it showed that we could make about a million dollars in guarantees during the first month, and that was not including our merchandise sales, which could possibly be more than that. That was just for the first month of touring, and the agents suggested that we do a second month of shows, which could earn us an additional million in guarantees.

Now, by 2016 standards, this could have been seen as a massive amount of money, or a rather small amount, depending on the kind of rock band you are talking about. The biggest rock bands in the world can command a million dollar guarantee for just one show, so by that standard, our tour was probably not very big. But for the Screaming Trees, who hadn't been an active band in over 15 years, this was a huge amount of money for us to be offered. Making two or three million dollars in just a couple months was more money than the band had probably made in its entire existence. That's the financial power of the so-called "legacy bands," who can cash in on their previous reputation for classic rock nostalgia.

The morning came when we were supposed to give our agents the "all-go" to pull the trigger and start confirming the show dates. I opened my email that morning to find a message from Mark, copying everyone and saying that he wanted to cancel the tour. No explanation was given, and I suppose none was to be expected—Mark often turned on a dime for reasons known only to him. Maybe he remembered his addiction during the 1990s and didn't want to be triggered again, or maybe he wanted to do something entirely different.

I must admit that I was pretty upset with the cancellation because it was Mark who had called to tell me about that festival offer in the first place. Plus, I had been doing all the liaison work with the booking agents, coordinating where the band would rehearse, who might be on the crew, and all the details that are required of this sort of venture. Then I thought about it from a different perspective.

All truly great bands are destined to break up, and the greatest bands in history only lasted a relative handful of years: The Beatles (7 years), Led Zeppelin (12 years), The Clash (10 years), Nirvana (7 years).

The Screaming Trees had lasted for 15 years, and maybe it was better and certainly much cooler that we didn't get back together like every other band from that time. Plenty of legacy bands continue to do those reunion tours, and the vast majority of the time, it's a pale representation of what they once were.

In the end, the Screaming Trees decided to be remembered as a fireball in the sky, rather than a Las Vegas casino act.

COVID DREAMS

The last time I physically saw Mark was in 2013, when he was playing a solo show at the Neptune Theatre in Seattle. I had seen him there once before and he had invited me to the show, putting me on the guest list. It was one of his mesmerizing acoustic shows, with his superb guitarist, Jeff Fielder, accompanying him on just a single acoustic guitar. After the show, there was a merchandise table where Mark would be signing books and LPs for his numerous fans. I was in the process of leaving the building when I saw Mark approach the table, so I walked up to say hello. One of the security guard goons from the theater tried to put me in a chokehold, which I wrestled free from, right as someone yelled, "Let him go, it's Bear from the Trees you idiot!" I guess Mark was worried about big guys approaching him so he had extra security that night.

Mark, noticing the commotion after that fact, looked up and shook my hand as I approached the table. "Hey bro, that was an amazing show as usual. I just wanted to say hello before we leave," I said. Weirdly, Mark didn't seem to recognize me, which was disconcerting because I had just been in the studio with him a few months earlier playing drums on his *Imitations (2013)* solo album. He seemed to be in a kind of confused daze, from what I can't imagine, but it didn't sit well with me.

It was exactly five years later, and somewhat out of the blue, when Mark emailed me again to ask if I would sing back up vocals with him on another show he was doing in Seattle. I wrote back that I would love to sing with him, but I was about to leave for the Amazon Rainforest, this time with my wife, where I was going to record another album for the Shipibo Shamans. There was no way I could make the show, and sadly, my last memory of seeing Mark in person was at that 2013 Neptune Theatre show.

In the summer of 2021, I had just finished producing an album with three prominent American songwriters: Peter Buck, Rich Robinson from The Black Crowes, and the singer, Joseph Arthur. I was the drummer, upright bassist, engineer, and producer. Although the album has still not been released for scheduling reasons, it was recorded during that awful period of time that everyone refers to as "The Pandemic," or "The Lockdown." I started calling it "The Covid Dream" because it was a period of great trauma, a real nightmare for many people, and most of us lost someone we knew during that horrific time. However, it was also a period of great creativity and reflection for many, and I was no exception. I produced a handful of albums in my home studio during this time, including the album I've just described here.

I was preparing the final mixes for the mastering engineer, but the sequence of the album was still undetermined. This was made more complicated by the fact that the album is a double album with 18 songs, all of which had to fit perfectly on the four sides of two vinyl LPs. The sequence had been left to me because Peter, Rich, and Joseph had no desire to take on the task.

A big part of sequencing an album is math, where you consider the length of the songs and a few other technical variances that make it all fit together. But sequencing is really an art form, and few people were as good at it as Mark Lanegan. Since Mark and I had sequenced all of the Trees albums, I emailed him to see if he could help.

Mark wrote back that he had been in the process of moving to Europe when the pandemic stranded him in Ireland, where he had to remain under the country's lockdown protocols. I emailed him the album as a digital download, and since he knew all of the musicians in the band, I asked if he could help sequence it. He emailed me back the following day, saying that he absolutely loved the album and would be enjoying it for quite some time. This was something Mark never said about any of the albums I had sent him over the years, so I took it as a good sign.

A few days later, Mark gave me an album sequence that worked perfectly and lined up exactly across the four sides of the two LPs, so we mastered the album exactly as Mark had sequenced it. This back and forth conversation ultimately led Mark to telling me the story of his hospitalization for Covid, something I had been completely unaware of until then.

Mark and I wouldn't talk for months or even a year at a time, but then we'd pick up right where we had left off, as if no time had passed. I was shocked to hear how severe his case of Covid had been, and how he had spent nearly three months in an Irish hospital, and the better part of a month on a ventilator. It was pretty much a miracle that he had survived at all.

I had spent the lockdown writing my third book so I sent that to Mark in an email, and that's when Mark emailed me a draft of his final book, *Devil In A Coma (2021)*. He asked me to give him some editorial comments before he finished his final draft, which I did. It's an incredible book about the spiritual visions he had when he was on the ventilator in an Irish hospital, barely alive, and stuck between the realms of life and death. I highly recommend it for anyone who wants a real window into Mark's soul.

I love that Mark and I always had this literary connection between us, going back to the early days of the Trees when we were on tour, and we would swap books on the tour bus. Books like *Moby Dick (1851), or* a collection of short stories by Charles Bukowski, or the classic Cormac McCarthy western, *Blood Meridian (1985)*, which was the first book that Mark ever gave me. Somehow, *Blood Meridian* always stands out as the book that reminds me of the Screaming Trees on tour, as if we were in some kind of parallel story, living the exaggerated myth of the Screaming Trees.

It was just a few months after that when I had my last interaction with Mark. I was producing the soundtrack for a delta blues documentary, the blues being something that Mark and I both loved. I mean, to be frank about it, Mark was essentially a blues singer at his core.

I asked Mark if he might want to record a delta blues cover for the soundtrack, and he ended up sending me two—both by the great blues singer, Blind Willie McTell. Mark recorded his vocals directly into his cell phone, emailing me the raw vocal tracks. He told me that I could add any music I wanted to his vocals, but his voice by itself was so beautiful, I didn't want to touch them. Jack Endino and I mixed them for the soundtrack, and we left them just exactly as they were, his raw voice penetrating the air with no musical accompaniment. Mark's voice was perfect just by itself, and anything added would have lessened the impact.

It was only two months later, on February 22nd, 2022, that our spiritual, musical brother passed from this physical realm to a place that I hope is more peaceful than the one he left behind. A huge void was etched into the hearts of those who knew Mark, and the world seems like an emptier, lesser place without him.

It was as if an ancient tree, which had seen the best and the worst in men, yet still survived, only to finally be cut down.

THE CLASSROOM AT
THE BACK OF THE BUS

When I think back on my time in the Screaming Trees, I now see that it was our Promethean courage that would never allow us to give up. But we also carried the curse of Sisyphus, who cheated death, and then was sentenced to roll a boulder up a mountainside, for eternity.

In the decade I spent on the road with the Trees in the 1990s, and the additional two decades since, what I remember most about our time together are those years on the tour bus, rolling down the endless highways of the world, through the night and into the sunrise. We had some time off here and there, but when I pieced together the timeline for this book from 1991 to 2016, it felt like I had lived an entire lifetime in the Screaming Trees.

All of that talking, and laughing, and listening to music in one bus, with a small crew of guys who, aside from a couple replacements here and there, generally remained the same. We drove and flew across hundreds of thousands of miles in North America, Europe, and Australia, and miraculously, all of us made it home alive.

The back of the bus became a kind of musical sanctuary for everyone because we often didn't get hotel rooms unless we had a night off. Most nights after a show, we just rolled out of town and kept going, driving through the night to the next city, and then we'd set up the whole circus, all over again. It was during those all-night drives when I would chose one of two spots on the bus—either up front in the jump seat next to the driver, where I'd put on my headphones and unwind, listening to the music of Miles Davis or John Coltrane. Or I'd sit in the back of the bus with Mark, John Hicks, Danny Baird, and sometimes even the Conner brothers would join as well.

Generally, the brothers held court in the front of the bus, where we'd watch classic movies on VHS tapes taken from their family video store. John Hicks would venture forward to add his impersonations and comedic commentary to the films, which was his appointed duty. This is where I learned a great deal about cinema, just from watching films and riding that all-night bus into oblivion.

We all agreed that Francis Ford Coppola's, *Apocalypse Now* (1979) was the greatest movie ever made, mainly because every aspect of a man's character is depicted in that film. We also ranked John Carpenter's, *The Thing* (1982) as a close second for the very same reasons. Almost every member of the band and crew could recite those movies, line by line.

Sometimes a member from an opening band would join us for a short leg of the tour, and then we would all be sitting there watching movies in the front, and listening to music in the back, to every great film and every great album ever made up to the late 1990s. That's when the back of the bus became a classroom for me, and for us all.

You see, despite everything I've told you about the Screaming Trees in all of these stories, including the hilarious and the horrible, the fact remains that we were all great musicians and songwriters whose diverse talents became something much more powerful. It became like a science laboratory for music.

I had gone to college to study jazz and classical music—none of the other Trees had done that, yet together they could write songs that our fans will remember for the rest of their lives. One time, Mark asked me to recommend some jazz albums to send to his father for Christmas, which I was able to do easily. But I was also unaware of much of the American and European songbook that had laid the foundation for everything the Trees would build upon. Looking back on it, I was indeed the naïve kid who had the good luck to join a band like the Trees, and that's when my real schooling began.

Mark thought of me as this big, goofy kid with a huge head of hair and equally huge ideas about music, but for example, I had no real knowledge of the Velvet Underground, or The Ramones, or Joy Division. To be honest, I had listened to those bands, but they didn't really appeal to me the way jazz did. Admittedly, my own musical scope was limited, and it was the Trees who expanded my horizon. "This is the cool stuff man, this is the real songwriting" they would say, and that's all that really matters when it comes to making great albums, the songwriting.

It was Mark, Van, and Lee who started playing those albums for me, teaching me about the music I wasn't taught in music school, and it all took place in that classroom in the back of the bus.

I wasn't a music hipster when I joined the Trees, and I'll never be one in the future—that was never my goal. But damn, can I spot a great song when I hear it, and I learned all of that from being in the Screaming Trees.

When we started doing those big tours in 1992, every album ever made was being reissued on CD. We bought those CDs constantly, filling shopping bags, every time we stopped the bus near a record store or a truck stop because truck stops had huge CD selections back then. We bought CDs from new bands, all the classic bands, and all the reissues, of every musical genre imaginable. We listened to the British Invasion bands of the 1960s; African recordings from Fela Kuti in the 1970s; every European new wave band from the 1980s; and all the hardcore and punk bands that had started the American alternative movement that was still very new at the time.

We went through every single album from the classic rock era, and to be honest, I hadn't even listened to most of the Led Zeppelin catalog until I climbed aboard that bus. For drummers, John Bonham of Led Zeppelin is the Holy Grail, but I hadn't even studied *The Great One* until Mark pulled out a copy of *Physical Graffiti (1975)* and said, "You gotta listen to this one, son." I was already 25 when I became obsessed with Led Zeppelin, which is about the same age that the members of Led Zeppelin were when they made that album.

And then there was the delta blues, something the Trees all connected with at a spiritual level. I mean, if you listen to any Trees song, you can hear the blues in every single note of it. We played those delta blues albums every time we drove through the American South because the landscape seemed to cry out for it.

After the Trees finally ended, I went on to work with some actual blues legends, like Cedell Davis and Ironing Board Sam, where I played drums on multiple albums that were recorded in the Mississippi Delta between 2002 and 2015. This was an entirely new education for me, which I received from the foundational fathers of the blues, the original music form that rock & roll is built upon. It was because of Cedell Davis that I met my future wife, at one of his shows in New York, which was the very last show I ever played with him before he passed. That was the greatest gift Cedell could give me—the introduction to my future wife.

And the very last thing I worked on with Mark was that blues soundtrack in 2021. I guess it was perfectly appropriate that the blues would be our starting point, and also the last thing we worked on together.

A lot of what the Trees played on the bus was generally what you might call *folksinger music*. We listened to Bob Dylan, Dave Van Ronk, Gordon Lightfoot, Townes Van Zandt, Nick Drake, Leonard Cohen, Tim Hardin, Tim Buckley, Jeff Buckley, Patti Smith, Joni Mitchell, and of course, all the outlaw country artists like Waylon Jennings, Merle Haggard, Willie Nelson, Johnny Cash, and George Jones.

There were four songs that I distinctly remember Mark loving enough to sing along to in their entirety, and one of those songs was, "Reason To Believe," (1966) by Tim Hardin, a rather obscure but brilliant songwriter from the 1960s. Tim was also a Pacific Northwest musician, born in Oregon and joining the Marines before eventually settling into being a folksinger. Mark really loved that song, and Tim Hardin in particular.

Another song was, "Shanty Man's Life," (1964) by Dave Van Rock. It's another one of those classic American folk songs that is extremely haunting, especially in it's original recording.

The third song, which always stood out to me as one of the greatest songs ever written was, "He Stopped Loving Her Today," (1980) written by Bobby Braddock and Curly Putman, and recorded by the legendary country singer, George Jones. This really is a classic, and it's sung by one of the greatest singers of all time, of any genre. Anyone who ever starts a band should be required to listen to this song because it's such a masterpiece that even a hardcore punk band could play it, and it would still sound like a classic.

The last song is the song I most associate with the Screaming Trees because the music and lyrics seem to capture everything about who we were. That song is, "Gentle On My Mind," (1967) written by John Hartford, but most famously recorded by Glen Campbell. Glen had been a Wrecking Crew studio musician who played on Beach Boys albums, and later reinvented himself as a brilliant singer and guitarist. Now, a song title with the word "gentle" in it seems a bit incongruous for a band like the Screaming Trees, especially after all the stories I've told here. But the truth is, inside each of us was a soul looking for peace, and that song seemed to bring it every time.

I remember hearing Mark singing those songs, beginning to end, multiple times, and they never got old. In fact, every single member of the Screaming Trees and our crew could sing those songs. It was a magical time because every real artist knows when he or she hears the gold, and the Trees were always mining for it.

In so many ways, I owe my real music education to the Screaming Trees for playing all that incredible music, which amounted to tens of thousands of individual songs, spread out across thousands of albums. Being in the Trees made me truly love music, so much so that I would risk my life to do it, or at the very least, choose a life that meant there was no turning back *after* music.

What Mark Lanegan and the Conner brothers taught me, was that the pantheon of great songs was as equally important as the pantheon of great literature, or great films, or great art. And when it came to songs, they taught me to look for the lesser-known and more obscure artists, because artists who go for the best songs over commercial success always write the best ones. It's also why a great song stays in your memory forever, and the flavor of the month pop star fades into obscurity with each passing year.

And there is one gospel truth that I've learned about music in all of these decades, and it is this:

The best songwriters in almost every genre of music won't be heard on the radio, and they almost never have mainstream success. This is because most of what you hear on the radio now, and for the last 100 years or so, has mostly been paid for through various forms of payola. That is an indisputable, historical fact, which doesn't mean that some of those songs aren't great—many of them are. But they've also been paid for by the record labels, and most of them shouldn't even be there.

What is also true, perhaps as a corollary to the previous truth, is that great artists will always find a way to make unique and original recordings, whether they have a record deal or not, and whether they get played on the radio or not. The best of these records are usually not in the average person's record collection, but the musicians know who made those records, and we seek them out with a passion.

That was the atmosphere in the back of the Screaming Trees tour bus in the 1990s, with all that incredible music, saturated in every kind of booze, and occasionally with drugs, as we chain-smoked our way across the landscapes of the world.

I barely slept back then, I was so excited to be young and alive, playing music for people who loved music just as much as we did. The Screaming Trees were definitely the roughest, toughest, most hell-raising rock band that I ever played with, and yet they were great artists with a deep sensitivity to know what was truly great in music. That kind of life can only be survived in measured doses, because even with our young, twenty-something bodies, it took an iron constitution to pull off what we did. And for most of the 1990s, the Trees did it like no other band could. Until we couldn't.

I'd like to finish with the single most important thing I have earned from all of those years, something I'm still learning to this day, and it is this:

Always listen to the spirit of a song, first. Listen for its soul, and pay attention to the words that are being sung and what the artist is trying to say. Look for the interesting and unusual ideas that propel the music because it's always about the soul of the song, first and foremost. A song has it's own life, its own spirit, and a great artist will always convey that. If you look for that spirit, you'll find other like-minded artists who honor that timeless credo, just as Orpheus did when he defied the gods with songs that were deemed to be too beautiful for humans. That's because a great song is life itself, and a great song gives people meaning to their lives, by relating similar feelings and emotions that connect across time.

So if you're courageous enough to take up the sacred path of a musician, or even braver to become a songwriter, make damn sure that when you put a song down on tape for the whole world to hear, make sure you do absolutely everything within your power to make that song as magical as it can be. Capture its spirit, harness its blazing beauty, and make it come *alive.*

Because the world has plenty of mediocre songwriters, that's for sure, and you can find most of them on the radio tonight. But when your time is up and it's time leave this realm, nobody is going to care about your placement on the radio chart.

They're going to care about the songs you wrote, the songs which gave people a reason to believe.

EPILOGUE

Mark Lanegan made 8 studio albums with the Screaming Trees, 2 albums with Mad Season, various appearances with Queens Of The Stone Age, and 12 solo albums. He played countless shows in multiple countries all over the world, collaborating with multiple bands and solo artists along the way. He also wrote 4 books of stories and poems, including the definitive book on rock & roll excess, *Sing Backwards And Weep*. Mark passed away at his home in Killarney, Ireland on February 22, 2022.

Van Conner made 8 studio albums with the Screaming Trees, and 5 studio albums with his subsequent rock band, Valis. He also toured as the bassist for Dinosaur Jr., and later started the Seattle recording studio known as, *Strange Earth*, where numerous artists still record to this day. He had three children, and continued to make music from his home in Washington State until his death on January 18, 2023.

Gary Lee Conner made 8 studio albums with the Screaming Trees, and has recorded 7 solo albums to date. He has, by his own estimate, written about 500 songs, a practice that he does daily. Lee never toured again after the Screaming Trees, although he continues to write songs and produce solo albums from his home in San Angelo, Texas where he lives with his wife and daughter.

Barrett Martin made 4 studio albums with the Screaming Trees, 2 albums with Mad Season, 9 albums with Tuatara, and 10 albums to date with his solo group. He has written 4 books about music and culture around the world, as well as several short stories that have been published in magazines and newspapers. He holds a masters degree in ethnomusicology and linguistics, and was a professor of music for 7 years. His work as a producer, drummer, percussionist, and composer can be heard on over 150 albums, including several film and television soundtracks. As a producer and engineer, he has done recordings on 6 continents and in numerous countries, winning Latin Grammys and writing awards along the way. When he's not traveling or touring, he lives in Olympia, Washington with his wife where they operate a recording studio and production company.